ANOTHER SEASON

ANOTHER SEASON

A COACH'S STORY OF RAISING AN EXCEPTIONAL SON

Gene Stallings
and Sally Cook

Little, Brown and Company

Boston   New York   Toronto   London

First Edition

Library of Congress Cataloging-in-Publication Data
Stallings, Gene.
Another season : a coach's story of raising an exceptional son /
by Gene Stallings and Sally Cook.
p.   cm.
ISBN 0-316-81196-3 (hardcover)
1. Stallings, John Mark, 1962–   —Health.   2. Down syndrome—
Patients—United States—Biography.   3. Down syndrome—Patients—
United States—Family relationships.   I. Cook, Sally.   II. Title.
RC571.S73S73   1997
616.85′8842′0092—dc21
[B]   97-6112

10   9   8   7   6

MV–NY
Published simultaneously in Canada by Little, Brown & Company
(Canada) Limited

Printed in the United States of America

For Johnny
and for all of his special friends in Alabama
— G. S.

For Bob, Lizzie, and Alex
and for my mother and father
— S. C.

It is not enough to give the handicapped life, they must be given a life worth living.

HELEN KELLER

CONTENTS

▼

1	Champions	3
2	Johnny's Birth	12
3	College Station	44
4	Tough Times	68
5	Big Wins / Little Victories	78
6	Discovering the Pros	107
7	School Days	140
8	Cardinal Years	166
9	Transformed in Tuscaloosa	187
	Epilogue: A Dream Fulfilled	211
	Acknowledgments	214

ANOTHER SEASON

CHAPTER 1

CHAMPIONS

I HEARD the chant of thousands of Alabama football fans thundering throughout the huge New Orleans Superdome — "Rol-l-l, Tide!" The cheerleaders screamed, "How do you spell Sugar Bowl?" "B-A-M-A!" came the fans' deafening reply. "How do you spell national champions?" the cheerleaders yelled. The entire stadium seemed to quake as the fans cried, "B-A-M-A," taking time to give equal weight to each letter.

I loved these college fans. Their wild cheering always made my pulse race, only increasing my desire to win. And tonight, the first night of the new year, 1993, it was no different. We were competing against the University of Miami Hurricanes at the Sugar Bowl in New Orleans. The Alabama fans had been cheering nonstop for a good half an hour before the game had even started. And now the roar in the enclosed dome was so loud that it sounded as though an airplane were just about to land inside the stadium.

Not only was this the biggest college football game of the year, it was probably the most important game of my thirty-five-year

3

coaching career. We were regarded by the news media and other teams and coaches as the country-boy Davids taking on the big-city Goliaths. I'd read comments from the press that our team was too small and slow, that we were one-dimensional, that we could run but couldn't complete enough passes to win. And they were saying that the Hurricanes' Heisman Trophy–winning quarterback, Gino Torretta, would easily be able to throw against our defense. All week Miami's players were boisterous, smug and confident they'd win. They bad-mouthed and taunted our guys. "You don't have a chance. Go back home!" they yelled, whenever our players left our hotel.

At press conferences the media said that oddsmakers had made us the eight-point underdog. Of course, I replied to anybody who would listen, "I'll take my team any day, I think we're better." Sure, I was going out on a limb when I said that, but that's what I believed. There was just no question that our players wanted to win. As I watched them practice I could see the no-nonsense look in their eyes.

In the days leading up to the game, I noticed a change in the players' behavior. In the locker room, before and after practices, they were quieter and calmer than usual, and more focused. And even though our hotel was in the heart of New Orleans, only two blocks from the nightlife of the French Quarter, not one of them was late for curfew. Some players didn't even leave their hotel rooms at night. Despite what most everybody said — that we didn't have a prayer of winning — I knew we had a good shot.

This isn't to say that I wasn't anxious. I was fifty-seven years old and the head coach of the University of Alabama football team. I had been there for only three years, in a position that represents over one hundred years of tradition. Football is practically a religion in Alabama, and the team is the pride of the state. This is the way it's been since 1892, when the first game was played in Tuscaloosa.

Thirty years after that, in Philadelphia, Alabama defeated Penn State 9–7, for the first time bringing us national recognition by defeating a team from the Northeast. Four years later, when Alabama defeated Washington 20–19 in the Rose Bowl, a precedent was established. For the first time, sportswriters were taking a Southern football team seriously. Over the years Alabama had gone on to win eleven national championships and had made an unprecedented forty-five bowl appearances in postseason play. Now our fans *expected* to win; they wouldn't have it any other way.

And, of course, the legendary coach, Paul "Bear" Bryant, was a tough act to follow. I've always said that everybody in the state loves Coach Bryant and they tolerate the rest of us. Coach Bryant won more games than any other coach in college football Division I-A history. He had an average of 9.3 wins per season during his twenty-five years as coach of Alabama. I remember Coach Bryant saying, "I ain't nothin' but a winner." I once heard him tell a reporter, "If wanting to win is a fault, as some of my critics seem to insist, then I plead guilty. I like to win. I know no other way. It's in my blood."

He was a true hero in the South and instilled pride in a state that ranked among the nation's poorest and worst educated. When he arrived at Alabama, in 1958, the team had won only four games in the previous three years. He didn't waste much time changing things, and by the 1960s and seventies he was the winningest coach in the country. His picture was on the cover of national news and sports magazines regularly, and I was amazed as I watched the newspapers' sports sections in Alabama double and triple in size to cover Coach Bryant and his team. People were fascinated by what he was thinking, doing, and saying.

But even though I was considered part of the Alabama family — having played for Coach Bryant at Texas A&M and then worked as an assistant coach for him with the Tide for seven years — there had still been a lot of public skepticism when I was hired for the job.

In fact, when I was named head coach of Alabama a lot of people were just plain shocked because I didn't have a very good record. My previous head coaching positions, at Texas A&M and in the NFL with the St. Louis and Phoenix Cardinals, had been full of ups and downs. It had been a roller coaster with tough recruiting, big wins, and sudden firings.

After the announcement that I would become Alabama's twenty-second head coach I remember how newsmen surrounded me and bombarded me with questions. I told every one of them that I knew my record wasn't what I would have liked, but that our teams would be very competitive. We were going to have a good season. They would see.

Well, we lost our first three games that year, first to Southern Mississippi, then to Florida and Georgia. Things were about as tense as they could be. The fans were furious that we were 0–3 and sports-writers began writing negative things about me in their columns, questioning whether I had been a good choice. But fortunately things started to turn around and we beat two important rivals, Tennessee and Auburn, finishing up with a 7–5 season and going on to the Fiesta Bowl. Then the next year we lost only one game and finished up ranked in the top five. Still, it had been thirteen long years since Alabama had won a national championship. Optimism was not particularly high. But as usual it was assumed that we would win. You better believe the pressure was on tonight.

The cheering in the stadium continued to grow louder, and I paced up and down the sideline watching each play carefully. At halftime, my mind wandered briefly to a few hours earlier. I thought about leaving my hotel suite at the Riverwalk Hilton by myself. My wife, Ruth Ann, and the children had gone to the stadium an hour before me because I stayed behind to go over last-minute details with two of my coaches, Mike Dubose and Woody McCorvey. When

I left my suite and came down to the lobby there were thousands of fans packed in there, eight and ten rows deep, cordoned off by police tape and cheering wildly. The two state troopers assigned to guard and assist me during the season, Captain Mike Sullivan and Lieutenant Cary Sutton, led me through the crowd and we boarded the bus to the stadium.

As I sat on the bus, riding down Canal Street through New Orleans headed toward the Sugar Bowl, I thought about my thirty-year-old son, John Mark. Earlier in the day he sat with me in our hotel suite during my pregame radio show. Johnny always enjoyed listening as I answered routine questions about different players, any injuries they might have, and my predictions for the upcoming game. Afterward he and I ate our usual little snack of peanut butter and crackers. But as he picked up his crackers I noticed how blue the tips of his stubby fingers looked. I'd seen this blueness at the ends of his fingers many times before, but today his fingers had such a deep blue hue they appeared to be almost purple. And it may have been my imagination, but Johnny seemed to be gasping for his breath. I had been worried but never got a chance to tell Ruth Ann, because of my preoccupation with the upcoming game. And now, in the midst of everything, I remembered this with alarm.

I clenched my jaw and folded my arms across my chest and looked out onto the field, and abruptly my thoughts returned to the game as we began the second half. On Miami's first possession, we intercepted Gino Torretta's pass, and a few plays later scored a touchdown. On the next Miami possession, cornerback George Teague intercepted yet another Torretta pass and scored. Teague then ran down receiver Kevin Williams and stripped the ball away on the next Miami possession. Our defense, amazing everyone, spurred us to a 27–6 lead. I heard a muted mumble jumble of words over the loudspeaker system and recognized the voice of the sportscaster Jerry Romig announcing the beginning of the fourth quarter.

We were playing really well, but I've been in this business long enough to know that just about anything can happen in the last minutes of a game. The Hurricanes returned a punt 78 yards for a touchdown to cut the lead to 27–13, but we responded with a twelve-play drive that ended when Derrick Lassic scored his second touchdown of the game and put the game out of reach. The fans went crazy. I looked up into the stands, into the glow of the stadium lights, and watched as they stood, waving and clapping their hands wildly. There was an electricity in the air that I had never felt before. I glanced at the clock. One minute forty-six seconds to go. Now I knew we were about to bask in the glory of a win — our thirteenth that year — and most likely the national championship.

When the game ended I found myself enveloped by a sea of crimson jerseys. Now I really appreciated how our team got its nickname — the Crimson Tide. Back in the early 1900s our defensive line was referred to as the Thin Red Line because of the team's crimson jerseys. Then, in 1907, when Alabama was playing during a torrential rainstorm and the team was covered in mud, a sportswriter reported that the players looked like a swarming crimson tide rolling down the field. Now the wild cheers of "Rol-l-l, Tide!" drowned out any other sound. In fact, the stadium was almost shaking with the cheers of the crowd as they chanted and screamed. I felt myself being hoisted onto the players' shoulders as they carried me off to the center of the field. For the first time all week I was relaxed and I began to enjoy the moment.

"We love you, Coach!" shouted one of the team members, waving his crimson helmet in the air. "We're number one," the others chanted, pointing their index fingers skyward as they carried me across the field. I was pelted with water and Gatorade from all sides. My sports jacket clung to my white shirt. The cold water felt great and I laughed out loud as I thought how my brand-new jacket would be ruined and probably have to be replaced. I would gladly go out and buy another one next week. As I was paraded to the center of the field, police and other players formed a barricade around the horde of photographers and fans trying to get close enough to shake hands or just to touch us.

Finally, the players lowered me and ran ahead into to the locker rooms. As I followed behind them, I thought back to all the times I had imagined what it must feel like to be in this position. But I never thought for one moment it would feel this gratifying. It had been one sweet year, and I couldn't believe that we were going to be national champions — for the twelfth time.

I couldn't wait to get to my family and celebrate with them a little more. As I walked into the locker room all 135 players knelt, and we all quietly said the Lord's Prayer together, just as we did after every game. Then the celebration began. Four or five players were hugging all at once, congratulating one another. Players were hollering, some were singing. Coaches, doctors, and people from the university were shaking hands, picking each other up and twirling around. We were ecstatic. It was even better than winning the lottery.

After fifteen minutes of reveling, it was time for my press conference. As I walked into the media room the print media, newspaper reporters and magazine writers from all over the country who stood impatiently over to one side, didn't bother me. The television people were buzzing around the room, setting up their heavy equipment and glaring lights. The bright camera lights and loud chatter flooding the room made me feel slightly dizzy. There must have been over three hundred media people squeezed into the room.

Suddenly there was a hush among the reporters as I walked up to the podium. I adjusted the microphone and people actually started applauding. I couldn't believe it. That kind of thing just doesn't happen that often. Finally I made a few short opening remarks, which consisted mostly of praising my players and coaches, and I took some questions from reporters. Then I quickly excused myself. I couldn't wait to see my family.

In a small cramped office next to the lockers and dirty uniforms that lined the floor, Johnny was waiting for me with my sons-in-law. We all hugged and shook hands. Then we visited for a few more minutes until one by one my four sons-in-law left the room. I sensed that they knew that Johnny wanted a turn to talk.

"Good job, Pop." Johnny grinned as he held his hand up for a high five.

My hand met his with a loud smack. I gave him a big old bear hug and we stood there together for what seemed like an hour. Johnny's head pressed up against my shoulder and I could tell that, just like his Pop, he was a little teary eyed. Barely five feet four inches tall, Johnny put his little arms around my waist and rested his head on my chest and squeezed me tight. I stroked my son's coarse light hair and looked down at his pale face. Those dark circles, which often showed up under his almond-shaped blue eyes and made him look sad and tired, were gone. He was smiling and laughing. When Pop was happy, Johnny was happy.

"We're going to be national champions, Johnny," I said. He looked up at me and gave me one of his sweet, adoring smiles. "That's big, son, real big."

It was the first quiet moment of the day. Johnny and I sat down next to each other on the couch in the corner of the room and I took his hand and squeezed it, thinking how much I'd enjoy seeing him wear one of those diamond-studded national championship rings. I looked at his hand and I looked down at mine. The tips of his short stubby fingers, the fingernails, tough and discolored, definitely looked bluer than usual. Johnny shivered slightly and cupped his hands over his mouth, a sign that he needed more oxygen. We'd go back to the hotel soon and Ruth Ann and I would put his oxygen mask on him. Johnny hadn't had much sleep in the last few days, with all of the excitement, but I knew that even though he was exhausted he'd want to stay up and celebrate with the players, coaches, and our friends. He'd want to hear us talk about the headlines of the next day's newspaper. Johnny was just stubborn that way.

Finally, he and I stood up together and headed for the door. As we walked hand in hand out onto the vast empty field, now dark and strangely quiet, and continued on toward the bus, I thought tonight how both of us had made it to places I had never dreamed possible. Of all of the thousands of sportswriters in this entire country, only one man, Corky Simpson, from Tucson, Arizona, had consistently voted us number one in the Associated Press polls and predicted that we'd win the national championship. And no one, not one doctor, not one friend, and certainly no one in our family, thought that John Mark Stallings would ever live to be thirty years old.

CHAPTER 2

▼

JOHNNY'S BIRTH

"WE'VE got the boy, Coach Bryant!" I practically shouted into the receiver, as I fumbled in my pockets to fetch another dime to drop into the hospital's pay phone slot. "Yes, she and the baby are just fine. Okay, I'll be sure to tell her that you and Mrs. Bryant send your best. Thank you. Goodbye." It was June 11, 1962. My wife, Ruth Ann, and I were elated. That evening, she had given birth to our son. We already had two beautiful, healthy girls. But it was no secret that we had now wanted a boy.

Every so often Coach Bryant would stick his head in my office and ask, "Say, when are you and Ruthie going to have a little football player?" As Coach Bryant's assistant at Alabama I was used to his occasional razzing. He had a knack for knowing exactly what was going on in a person's head, and I'm sure he must have realized how much Ruth Ann and I wanted a son. I'd get a flustered smile on my face when he'd start in, and I'd reply, "Real soon, I hope, Coach Bryant, real soon." But in the back of my mind I fretted that we might have a family of girls. Make no mistake, our daughters, Anna Lee and Laurie, were my pride and joy, but Ruth Ann and I also were really anxious to have a boy, there was just no question about that.

I'm sure the town of Paris, Texas, where I grew up, was no different from most small American communities in that sports was the main topic of conversation. I remember a pro baseball team called the Red Peppers came to Paris when I was in high school. The whole town rallied around that team, and my friends and I went to most of the games. There must have been one hundred of us standing out behind the bleachers. All of a sudden a batter would hit a foul ball and the people in the stands, sitting up high, would run to watch us as we fought and scrambled to get the ball, just so we'd get a free ticket into the game.

I loved sports and started playing football in the fourth grade. Our teams usually played for the city championship. In fact, I can't remember when I wasn't playing something. In the summer I was getting ready for football, then it was basketball, and in the spring I played golf. I was the captain of every team I had ever been on — both in high school and in college. The fun was always celebrating the wins and talking about the plays after a game. Sports were my life.

And now working for Coach Bryant got me used to the spotlight. When I'd be out of the office, in a restaurant or walking down the street, I'd hear people say, "There's one of Coach Bryant's assistants." Everybody in the state seemed to have their eyes on Coach Bryant, and if you were associated with him, they watched you, too.

One of the keys to his success was that people wanted to please him, and I was no different. When it became evident that he was leaving as head coach of Texas A&M and going on to Alabama as head coach, he called me into his office and said, "Now, I'm going to offer you a job on my staff in Alabama, but if I hear of it before I'm ready to announce it, then you don't have it."

Actually I wanted to run out and shout it from the rooftops. To be able to coach in a place like Alabama, well, that kind of thing doesn't happen very often, especially to a twenty-two-year-old, just out of college. Usually a guy starts out coaching high school and then works his way up. But the only person I told was Ruth Ann, until Coach Bryant made the announcement. I was tickled to death to have such a wonderful job and to be making forty-five hundred dollars a year!

Coach Bryant was in total control, and could he be intimidating! His coaches worked harder than most coaches, and the players practiced longer and harder than most players because they constantly wanted to please him.

Often, I dreamed of the day when my son would carry on the family tradition of playing football. Maybe he'd play for me and for Coach Bryant. There'd be times when I'd look at one of my players, and for an instant I'd see my imaginary son. He'd always be a big, strapping boy, and I'd envision him intercepting a pass, tucking that football under his arm, and sprinting for a touchdown. I'd be standing on the sidelines, so proud it would be hard to wipe the smile off my face.

I adored my daughters, Laurie and Anna Lee, three and a half and five years old, respectively. Even if I got home from work late (which seemed to be often these days, since Alabama had won the championship the previous season and we were gearing up for another great fall), Ruth Ann and the girls would wait for me to eat dinner with them. We had our fun little routines; every night before bedtime we always played the simple board game Parcheesi, and I'd find some way to let them win, whether it was positioning my player a few spaces behind what it should have been or re-rolling the dice to make certain it was a low number. Often the children would pedal an old surrey that we had bought several years before from a friend, while I'd run alongside. And though I'd never done any carpentry work before, Anna Lee and Laurie persuaded me to make them a toy box, helping me pound nails into the wood.

But I thought there'd be something a little different and special about my relationship with my son. Maybe we'd go fishing together and I'd teach him how to shoot baskets, or maybe we'd go off and watch a team like the Red Peppers and I'd buy him a ticket so he wouldn't have to catch a foul ball in order to get inside the gates. There was no end to what we could share together. Now on this evening of June 11, my dreams could become a reality. Our wish had finally come true.

The next morning I stopped at the florist on the main floor of the hospital and bought a small bouquet of yellow roses, Ruth Ann's favorite flowers. With the bouquet tucked securely under my arm, I strode confidently down the long, narrow corridor of Druid City Hospital, eager to see my wife and son. "Eugene Clifton Stallings III," I whispered to myself as I headed toward Ruth Ann's room. It was thrilling to think that I had a namesake. From the time we first got married Ruth Ann and I had always said that when we had a boy he would be named after my father and me — to carry on the family name.

I put the flowers behind my back as I walked into Ruth Ann's room. There she sat on the bed, her head propped up with pillows. Cards and flowers surrounded her. Even dressed in a drab green hospital gown she looked almost as young as the day I met her, eleven years before, when she was sixteen. My best friend, Gerald Jack, had always talked about his bright, pretty first cousin Ruth Ann. She and I were in a few classes together in high school and I was attracted to her right away. She was outgoing and popular, the editor of the student newspaper, the best French horn player in the state, capturing the All-State chair for three years, and the nicest girl in our tenth-grade class. For the next three years we were sweethearts, going out on dates after football games and helping each

15

other with homework assignments. I suppose we were considered the perfect couple by some folks in town. Ruth Ann was the homecoming queen her senior year in high school and I was captain of the football team. After we both graduated and went off our separate ways to college (I went to Texas A&M, in College Station, and she went on to East Texas University, in Commerce), we kept in close touch, writing letters to each other once a week. She'd often join my parents and come over from Commerce to an A&M football game. She graduated in three years and started teaching elementary school in Bryan, the next town over from College Station. We had wanted to get married before my senior year at A&M.

When I told Coach Bryant of our wedding plans he was adamantly opposed. "If you and Ruth Ann get married before the season you won't be able to live in the football dorm," he said. "You're one of the captains of the team and we need you in the dorm." He didn't have to say another word. Ruth Ann and I got married two days after the final A&M football game, the traditional Thanksgiving game when we played the University of Texas, our biggest rival. My teammates who played with me that Thursday, Jack Pardee, Dee Powell, and Bobby Drake, came to Paris to be in the wedding party. It was especially festive because A&M won the game.

When I looked around Ruth Ann's hospital room and noticed that the baby wasn't with her, I didn't think much about it. The nurses were probably dressing or bathing him. I kissed her and surprised her with the flowers. But she seemed distracted and set them on the radiator without unwrapping them. "Bebes," she began ("Bebes" is what she and all my close friends call me, the nickname my brother gave me as a child when he couldn't pronounce "Baby Gene"), "everyone else in the ward has seen their baby, but they haven't brought ours yet. Would you go out and ask the doctor if anything is wrong?"

Wrong? What could possibly be wrong? Only last night the doctor had popped his head outside the delivery room door and announced to me that we had a fine six-pound-one-ounce healthy baby boy. I had seen Ruth Ann right after she had delivered our son. She had been awake during the delivery and when I saw her, she was alert, ecstatic. I even got a peek at our baby boy through the nursery window, and I'd carried on with the lady next to me for quite a while about how sweet newborns look. That night I had telephoned just about everybody we could think of with the news.

Earlier in the morning I had stopped by my office and passed out cigars wrapped in cellophane with a baby blue band and an inscription that read, "It's a boy!" I'd been saving that box of cigars in my desk drawer for a long, long time. There had been a lot of backslapping and banter. The secretaries, coaches, and assistants were genuinely thrilled for us. Nothing could possibly be wrong. Ruth Ann must not have had much sleep. I hesitated for a minute and then I agreed to find the doctor.

It didn't take me long to locate him in the hallway. He was deep in conversation with some of the nurses. I walked over to him and waited until he finished talking. I felt a bit self-conscious as I asked if there was any kind of problem. "Yes, we think maybe your baby is a mongoloid," the doctor replied matter-of-factly. I was stunned, and then I got so mad at the coldhearted way the news was delivered that I drew back to hit him. I was going to knock that doctor right through the glass partition that led to the nurse's station. Instead I passed out before my fist could hit anything but the floor. It was a terrible shock, the furthest thing from my mind. When I came to, the nurses surrounded me and the doctor offered to talk to Ruth Ann.

I had to tell her, I knew that. I picked up my six-two-and-a-half frame off the floor and slowly headed back to Ruth Ann's room. The word "mongoloid" thundered in my head. It was such an awful-sounding term. Mongoloid. All I could think of was an ogre, or some kind of a monster. It wasn't until years later that "Down syndrome" replaced "mongoloid" as the accepted term.

17

A tight, painful knot formed in the pit of my stomach as I made my way to my wife's room. I paused at the door and watched as a nurse plumped up the pillows on her hospital bed. She and Ruth Ann were exchanging pleasantries. I lightly knocked on the open door and walked into the room. The nurse smiled politely as she rearranged some of Ruth Ann's clothes that were on the chair and then she turned and left. Ruth Ann was sitting on the side of the bed. Her brown hair was swept back off her forehead and fell loosely to her shoulders. Her soft green eyes met mine. "Are they going to bring the baby in?" she asked.

I knew I had to describe the doctor's diagnosis to her right away, but for a minute I couldn't speak. I wanted to tell her in a softer, more tactful manner than the way the doctor had told me.

"Ruthie," I finally said, taking her hands in mine and squeezing them, "the doctor just gave us some bad news." Ruth Ann began to cry and she let go of my hands. "I'm not real sure if he really knows, but he said there is something the matter with our little boy — that maybe he is retarded."

Ruth Ann couldn't believe what she was hearing. A fine, strapping football player was what she, too, had expected. "Oh, no, this can't be true, the doctor is mistaken. He can't be certain!" she said over and over again. For the first time in my life I felt totally helpless as I stood at the end of her bed and watched her sob. I walked over to the window, stared down at University Boulevard and the cars going by below.

All I could think of was Jack Horn, the big homely boy with the moon-shaped face who lived a few houses up the block from me when I was growing up in Paris. Jack probably had Down syndrome but we called him retarded. My pals hooted and hollered at him and we made fun of the way he stuck his thick tongue in and out of his mouth uncontrollably. We would run and act like we were scared of him because he looked so different. Now we had a son who was going to grow up to look and act just like Jack. Children would laugh at him and call him names. Maybe they'd scream and run from him, just like we used to do.

I gripped the windowsill and rested my forehead against the glass. I was still a little unsteady on my feet from passing out, and I started to feel nauseous. The cars and pedestrians five stories below seemed to be suspended in slow motion as I continued to stare out the window. Had I done something to cause this? I started thinking about the events of the last nine months. Maybe I should have listened a little more when Ruth Ann felt so tired those last few weeks. Or there was the possibility that something had happened during the last couple of hours before we got to the hospital. The baby was one month early; we hadn't expected him to arrive so soon. Even Ruth Ann didn't quite believe she was going into labor. I'd had to prod her to get going to the hospital, and she kept stalling as she insisted on ironing a dress for Laurie. Street noises flooded the room, making it impossible to think anymore.

Finally, the nurses brought our baby to us. My hands were unsteady as I carefully unwrapped the thin yellow blanket that covered him. I picked him up and when I cradled him in my arms I was surprised and pleased to find that he didn't look much different from other babies, maybe just a little paler. Ruth Ann and I explored his soft, fair skin, lightly touching each of his ten fingers and toes, his bald little head and his button nose, experiencing the same love and adoration we had felt when we held our daughters for the very first time. When I looked long and hard at his face I thought for a minute that I saw Ruth Ann's father's sweet and sincere expression in this child. He was a peaceful, precious newborn baby. We took turns holding him until the nurses came in and took him back to the nursery. Later that night we decided against naming him Eugene Clifton Stallings III. It was an agonizing decision, but we knew that he would never be able to carry on the family name and we thought that it would be more appropriate if he was given a biblical name. We decided on John Mark Stallings — Johnny for short.

Over the next few days Ruth Ann began to attribute Johnny's sleepiness and sallow skin to the fact that he was born one month prematurely. I was certain the doctors had made an error, and she was beginning to be convinced, too. "Doctors make mistakes just like everybody else," I told her. Just saying those words made me feel better. So over and over again I reassured Ruth Ann that Johnny wouldn't be any different from any other child. He sure seemed exactly like all the other babies I'd ever seen.

I could tell by Ruth Ann's icy stares and the short, clipped way she spoke to the doctors that she was beginning to be angry with them for trying to make her believe something about our baby that she thought couldn't possibly be true. A few days later we arrived home completely exhausted and without Johnny. He was so sleepy and pale that the doctors wanted to observe him and give him oxygen for a few days before releasing him from the hospital.

"Who has our baby brother?" Laurie tugged at my pants pocket as she asked me that question over and over again. Anna Lee started to wake up in the night and cry, something she hadn't done in a long time. With a forced cheerfulness, we told the girls that their brother needed a little extra attention and that soon he'd be home. We were determined to hide Johnny's condition from them because we were almost sure that the doctors were wrong.

Ruth Ann's mother, Mrs. Jack (the children called her Mammy), came the minute she heard Johnny was born, to help us out for a month. I honestly don't know what we would have done without her warmth and support. Mammy was an older grandmother — she was forty-three years old when Ruth Ann was born — and now she devoted herself to her grandchildren. Her husband, Ollie, a clothing salesman in Paris, had died when Ruth Ann was in college.

Mammy was a very calm person, with a charming sense of humor. She'd know just when to make a joke, and it was usually in the middle of a good deal of commotion at home. In 1910 she had graduated early from East Texas Normal School, in Commerce, Texas, which later became East Texas University. When she was eighteen years old she rode sidesaddle to a one-room schoolhouse and taught elementary schoolchildren. She had grit and determination and she was a magnet for all the children.

Whenever she walked into the room they ran to her, and she'd scoop them up in her arms and they'd settle on her lap and want every last bit of her attention. The children would tell her about their friends, school, their pets, and give detailed accounts of what was going on in their lives. In addition to cooking three meals a day and taking care of the cleaning, she played for long stretches with the girls. During that period Ruth Ann and I could hardly cope with the day-to-day routines of family life because we were both so deeply depressed and exhausted. Often, I'd wake up without sleeping more than two hours because I had been so restless and anxious. Then, on the days and nights when I'd be okay, Ruth Ann would be crying and having a bad time. Thank goodness, one of us seemed to be a little more up when the other person was down. We continually asked ourselves, "Why did this happen to us?" No one we knew had a child with Down syndrome and we knew nothing about it. Our only comfort was to say that the doctors had made the wrong diagnosis. At night, we prayed constantly that Johnny would become a normal child.

After a few days he was released from the hospital. But unlike our first two babies, he didn't cry very much and we often had to wake him to feed him. His sucking reflex was weak, and Ruth Ann tried hard but couldn't nurse him. Instead we fed him with a bottle that had a special free-flowing nipple.

Mammy was determined that Johnny was going to be as healthy and strong as he could be. She'd sit with him for hours until he finished all of his bottle. Often, she'd wake up for the nighttime feedings, and during the day she'd patiently sit and hold Johnny for hours while she happily watched the girls fuss over him. She would take her time bathing and dressing him. Most days she would walk Anna Lee to kindergarten and then take Laurie to her pre-school. When the girls got home they made up games where Johnny was their baby; he was in their eyes the most precious baby in the world. They found nothing different or wrong with their brother, and I think they were surprised because we were constantly reminding them that Johnny was fragile and they had to be very careful with him. But we were also mindful not to discuss Down syndrome in front of them. We were thrilled that they loved and accepted him as their cherished baby brother, and we never wanted them to behave differently.

Meanwhile, many of the doctors and some of our friends were pushing us to put Johnny in an institution because it would be "easier on the family." "The baby will become such a burden to your girls," said a friend.

"He will never sit, walk, or talk. I'm certain that you and Ruth Ann just aren't up to the demands that go along with raising this kind of child," said one of the doctors.

"He'll hinder your chances of being a successful coach," said another friend. This steady pressure on us was very upsetting, and we were unsure of what to do.

The only institution I knew even the slightest bit about was our state institution for retarded youngsters, called Partlow State School and Hospital. I drove past it every day on my way to work. It was just a stone's throw from the hospital where Johnny was born and located less than a mile from the university, on University Boulevard. Now when I drove past it I slowed down and carefully examined the columned red brick buildings that were set about a half mile back from the road, veiled by trees. If you didn't know it was there you could easily drive right past the huge wrought iron fence that separated the grounds from the street. You'd barely notice the wards and cottages beyond, where people lived in groups. It was pretty obvious that the patients were not meant to be seen by people driving by.

For the last few years Ruth Ann and I had been taking Billy Clear, a little boy who lived at Partlow, to church on Sunday mornings. Billy's grandmother had called our church, asking if anyone was willing to take him out of Partlow and over to church once a week. Since we had been married, we had always done some kind of volunteer work, and we were happy to meet a new little boy and take him to church with us. There was talk that Billy had deep emotional troubles and that he was sometimes incorrigible. I guess that's why he lived there, but he seemed like a typical little ten-year-old boy to me. He liked tossing a football and he ate real well at our Sunday lunch. He was a nice-looking little guy with big blue eyes and freckles. For the few hours that he was with us, he acted just fine.

When we would go over to Partlow on Sunday mornings to pick him up, the heavy-gauge metal doors would be locked and Billy would be peering out from the window of one of the cottages, his little fingers curled around the metal grates. Steel bars and metal grates partly concealed all of the windows. We had the feeling he was isolated and alone, almost like he was in a prison.

The stern uniformed guards, carrying a jangle of keys, would go through a series of unlocking doors when we arrived. Once we were in the building we were locked in tight. Right outside the wrought iron gates there was a tiled fountain surrounded by benches. Any time of the day when Ruth Ann and I were at Partlow, there were residents sitting on those benches with vacant looks in their eyes, their arms folded tightly across their chests. They'd be rocking back and forth, back and forth, as if they were in a trance.

I didn't know it at the time but I later found out that there was a serious problem with overcrowding at the institution. By the 1970s stories had started to appear in the state's newspapers on conditions in mental health and mental retardation facilities throughout Alabama. Eventually I found out that Partlow was in bad disrepair: the toilets didn't work, there were gaping holes in the ceilings, and the beds were so close together that you couldn't walk in between them. There was no access for fire engines, and the fireplug couplings were so old that they wouldn't fit modern-day hose couplings. They had no fire alarm system or sprinkler system. The whole place smelled like urine and sour milk, and a couple of journalists wrote of vomiting the minute they walked into the place because of the horrible stench. No wonder Billy became sullen and withdrawn every Sunday afternoon when we had to take him back.

One of the reasons I felt that people kept urging us to institutionalize Johnny was that there was a certain embarrassment among some folks when they had to confront a "retarded" child. And time has a way of curing things — if you put your child in an institution, maybe you eventually think it didn't happen, that you never had a child who was born disabled. You start off visiting a little bit, then you don't visit as much, and soon you're not sure whether you have a child with Down syndrome or not.

I stood firm: putting Johnny in an institution was just not an option. We were told that our son would look different and act differently, but we made a conscious choice that he was ours to love and we were going to try to make him into the best person possible. Our commitment was solid. We were going to take Johnny home, keep him happy and healthy, and we were going to love him, just as we did our daughters.

As a coach I have never had patience for Monday-morning quarterbacks. During games I've often had a few seconds at the most to make win-or-lose decisions. I was used to making these rapid-fire decisions and reaping the consequences, so I guess it wasn't at all surprising that we came to this choice quickly. Besides, doctors were telling us of what Johnny would *become*. But for now he was our sweet, delightful baby boy. When I'd get home from work at night I'd watch as Ruth Ann bathed him in the bathroom sink and I'd want to help. I would wrap him up in a towel, dry his little toes, and then Johnny would gaze up at me with his bright blue eyes. At those moments I'd feel so proud and pleased that I had such a sweet little son. There was just no question, John Mark Stallings was going to be a part of our family. That might have been against the norm, contrary to what our friends and the doctors were advising us, but when Ruth Ann and I talked, that was the decision we made.

For the first couple of months after we got Johnny home from the hospital I kept thinking that the doctors had made a mistake. I'd hold him in my arms for a while and say to Ruth Ann, "Why, this baby looks fine. Come on over here and take a look. There's absolutely nothing wrong with this boy." I kept up like that for months. In fact, Ruth Ann and I convinced ourselves that Johnny was "normal," and we became determined to prove the doctors wrong. We both dreamed about the day when we would walk into the doctor's office, hold Johnny up proudly, and say, "You see, he was fine all the time. You misdiagnosed him, probably because he was premature."

Most of our friends, with the exception of a few close ones, talked with us about everything except Johnny. Many times when we started to say something about him, they'd quickly change the subject. On the occasion when a friend or family member did ask how he was getting along, I usually told them what the doctors said, but I always added, "I think they're wrong." Yes, maybe Johnny's ears were a little bit smaller than other babies', and his eyes did look somewhat slanted. They were so clear blue that they didn't look real. The doctors pointed out that people with Down syndrome often have a gap between their big toe and second toe and an upward slant to the eyes. Johnny had these traits, too, but we couldn't see them, or we just didn't want to.

At the end of July, when Johnny was six weeks old, we finally gave in to the urging of our doctors and took him to Birmingham for a chromosome test, which would tell us definitively if he had Down syndrome. After a few long weeks of waiting, the results came back.

Most people can remember where they were when Neil Armstrong set foot on the moon, or when they heard that President Kennedy had been assassinated. I'll never forget where I was when Johnny's diagnosis was confirmed. As I sat drafting a letter to a recruit, the doctor called. His voice was low and serious and I was pretty certain of what he was about to say. But when I heard the words "The tests are conclusive. Johnny has Down syndrome," I felt detached and numb.

I closed the door to my office, asked my secretary to hold my calls, and sat silently for a good long time. I thought back to how ecstatic I had been for twenty-four hours after I first learned that I had a son. Those twenty-four hours were probably the happiest moments in my life. Now it was confirmed, Johnny would never be normal. Once again, I had to tell Ruth Ann something she didn't want to hear.

I sat at my desk motionless, as if in a trance, my head propped up between my hands, staring at a photograph of Ruth Ann and the girls on the wall. When I finally got up to go home I looked at my watch. It was 7:30 P.M., an hour later than when I usually left. I thought about calling Ruth Ann, like I always did whenever I was running late, but I just couldn't pick up the phone.

When I opened my office door, my secretary was gone and the hallways of the athletic offices were deserted. My footsteps echoed loudly through the corridors as I walked quickly out of the building to the car. It was now dark and I dug deep in my pockets for my car keys, discovering that I had left them and my briefcase back in the office. As I ran back into the empty building I tried to think of what

I was going to say to Ruth Ann. Over the last few months we had completely convinced ourselves that Johnny was a "normal" child. Now I look back on that time and wonder how we could possibly have let ourselves get caught up in such self-deception. We told each other all the time that Johnny was a premature baby and that eventually he'd be strong and big and look like other babies. As I slowly opened the back door I couldn't think of anything to say to Ruth Ann.

The minute I walked into the house I knew I should have called her. She and the girls had waited to eat dinner with me, and they all looked worried as Ruth Ann put the plates in the oven to warm them. Johnny was asleep and the four of us sat at the table and ate dinner in silence. Finally, I couldn't stand it anymore and I tried to be lighthearted, recounting a joke I had heard earlier in the week, but everyone seemed unusually subdued. Surely, they felt my sadness. After dinner we tucked the children into bed and then I told Ruth Ann about the doctor's phone call.

"Then, it's true, there's nothing we can do," she said. Her voice, usually so full of life, was dull and flat. I held her in my arms for a long time and we both cried. It was now a fact, Johnny had Down syndrome.

A few days later the doctor called us to his office and explained a lot more about Down syndrome. For the first time ever we learned that it was a genetic disorder in which a child is born with one extra chromosome that usually causes delays in physical, intellectual, and language development and is one of the leading causes of mental retardation in the world. The doctor explained that these children have some physical similarity to their parents, siblings, and grandparents.

Johnny had clear blue eyes exactly like Ruth Ann's daddy, and he and Anna Lee had very light complexions. His face was round just like Laurie's. But the doctor said that children with Down syndrome also share some common traits with other children who have the same chromosomal disorder. Some have only a few of these characteristics, while other children have many.

It seemed Johnny had the most common ones: his muscle tone was low and his head was more wobbly than most infants'. One of his ears was crinkly, and he had the simian crease, which was a single deep crease across the center of his palm, and a flat facial profile. Johnny had a somewhat depressed nasal bridge and a very small nose, all common characteristics of a baby with Down syndrome. The doctor then told us that although Down syndrome occurs in one out of every eight hundred to a thousand births, it was only ten years earlier, in the mid 1950s that methods of examining chromosomes had become available. In 1959, the French researchers Lejeune, Gautier, and Turpin discovered forty-seven chromosomes present in each cell instead of the usual forty-six. Then, it was later determined that an extra partial or complete twenty-first chromosome affects a person's physical and mental development.

We heard so many people say "Down's syndrome," but the preferred way of saying it is "Down syndrome," without the apostrophe and "s." An English physician, John Langdon Down, published an academic paper on the subject of mongolism in 1866, and he became known as the "father" of the syndrome. Today we know that children with Down syndrome are more like the average child than different. Just like all of us, these children feel deeply and want to form meaningful relationships and go out and socialize, and they want to learn and to be challenged. But in 1962 doctors overemphasized the differences.

As educated as I was becoming on the subject, I still felt that something like this just didn't happen to a guy like me. I had the job that I'd wanted more than anything else in the world. I mean, I actually believed things like this happened to people who had a lot fewer advantages than I did. All my life I thought that good things came my way because of a little luck and a great deal of hard work. But now I felt unlucky, and for the first time in my life I felt different from almost everybody I knew. My only son was disabled. I thought he would never be able to throw a football, go out on a date, or have children. Ultimately, we learned that any family can have a child born with Down syndrome, and it is not in any way related to one's race, nationality, religion, or socioeconomic status. But I had always thought that bad things like this only happened to other people.

I threw myself into my work. It seemed to be the only thing to help me cope. The season before, Alabama had gone undefeated and we had won the 1961 national championship. We were pushing hard for another great season, and recruiting top players was taking up most of my time. Working in such a demanding and competitive environment temporarily took my mind off the difficulties at home. There was always a constant stream of activity at our door — reporters, other coaches, players — and when things went well we got a lot of praise from alumni and fans. Working with talented young players was always stimulating for me. I could go to work for a few hours and I'd almost forget about the situation at home. At times it almost seemed like a bad dream. There were days when I'd head home from the office and I'd think to myself, "When I walk in the door I'm sure Johnny will be a normal child."

But even though work was a refuge for me, when coaches and friends stopped by my office to visit I felt an uneasiness in the air. Whenever the subject of Johnny's birth came up, I'd notice that people would lower their voices and shake their heads. One afternoon, all of the coaches had gathered for a meeting and I was running late. As I jogged down the hall I passed two secretaries talking near the water fountain who obviously didn't see me. I overheard one of them say, "They must have done something wrong, otherwise the baby would have been all right." I really couldn't get mad at what she said because in the back of my mind I thought that maybe I *had* done something wrong, even though the doctor had thoroughly explained Down syndrome's chromosomal origins.

It was tough facing my parents. My daddy had been in the roofing business in Paris, but things didn't work out for him and he later became a storm adjuster for an insurance company, traveling and working even longer hours than he had before. From the time my older brother, Jimmy, and I were little we tried to make our daddy proud of us. We grew up with a strong work ethic — Jimmy worked in retail stores and I was always mowing lawns, caddying at the Paris Country Club, or sacking groceries at the Piggly-Wiggly, our local market. Some summers I worked for Dad, repairing the shingles on roofs.

He constantly bragged about my being a coach at the University of Alabama. He was born in Alabama and later settled in Texas, but he remained a true Tide fan. Whenever he was driving on the Texas roads and he spotted a car with Alabama license plates, he'd follow that car until it pulled into a gas station or a diner and he'd say to the person, "Gee, I see that you're from Alabama. Well, my name is Gene Stallings. I just wanted to tell you that my son is a coach for the Crimson Tide." Dad never had the opportunity to go to college, and he loved walking around the Alabama campus and visiting me in my office.

My mother, in her early sixties, still worked for a title company in Paris. She was one of the few people in Paris who understood title abstracts. I can't remember a time when she didn't work. In fact, she was still typing letters at age ninety. Her employer wouldn't let her quit because she was so valuable to the company. Mother had a mind of her own. In fact, some people say that she and I were a lot alike. She was a proud woman and it was hard for her to admit that I had a difficult situation to deal with.

My parents first visited us in August just after Johnny's diagnosis was confirmed. They both held him for a short time and without saying too much handed him back to Ruth Ann and then fussed over the girls. At dinner that night, they both asked me endless questions about the incoming freshmen athletes and what kind of season Alabama was going to have. I found myself talking nonstop about my work and about Joe Namath, the second-year quarterback from Beaver Falls, Pennsylvania, whom everyone was watching. But my mother's expression was somber and I watched as she focused on Johnny, who was sleeping in Ruth Ann's arms. I wonder if Mother would be relieved for all of us if Johnny died, I thought to myself that night. Rather than admit that Johnny was different, she kept a distance. It wasn't because she didn't care. If anything, she cared too much. She so wanted him to be "normal" like the others because she wanted me to have a fine, healthy big son — a son who would carry on the Stallings name.

Almost every night when I came home from work I found Ruth Ann poring over articles and books, anything she could get her hands on to find out more about Down syndrome. She still wanted more information than the doctors could offer. The few books that were written on the subject shed little light on the extra chromosome and offered no explanation of the cause. And that's true even today. The causes and prevention are still unknown. But Ruth Ann was determined to find a reason for Johnny's disability. She was certain that she had done something wrong during her pregnancy, and she methodically reexamined each day she was pregnant and the several months before he was even conceived.

Just like most new parents we were eager for others to love our new baby and show their approval. Our friends and family had paid a great deal of attention to our two daughters when they were babies, coming over for visits, showering them with gifts and compliments. Now when we went out to dinner or on an outing and people walked over to us to say hello, they would give the girls a hug or a pat on the head, and then they would look at Johnny and, seeing his slanted eyes or the way his head drooped and how he drooled excessively, they'd realize that something was wrong. They would stop, back off, and say something superficial like, "Oh, isn't he cute?" This kind of thing happened time after time and I noticed that Ruth Ann started seating Johnny with his back toward people when we'd go out.

I wanted people to show some concern. I wanted them to ask all of the usual things that you ask when someone has an infant. I would have loved to hear, "Is he growing? Is he sleeping well through the night?" But instead, people would say, "I know how you feel." If one person said that to me, one hundred people did. I always wanted to answer, but I never did, "How could you possibly know how I feel? You haven't had a child with a disability." But when people didn't ask about Johnny, my feelings were just as hurt.

It would have been so much better if people had acknowledged that Johnny was different. Maybe we could have talked about it a little. I'm sure we all would have felt less frightened and intimidated. But instead we ended up with polite small talk and I'd feel embarrassed and detached.

During the first few weeks after Johnny's birth, Ruth Ann thought for sure that Coach Bryant's wife would come over and visit, but she never came and Ruth Ann was greatly disappointed. One day a messenger arrived at the door and delivered two beautifully gift-wrapped packages with a card that read, "Best Wishes, Coach and Mrs. Bryant." Mrs. Bryant had sent over a dress for Ruth Ann and a stuffed animal for Johnny. That was nice, but more than anything, Ruth Ann wanted her to say, "Ruthie, I'm thinking of you, I'm hurting for you." But for Mrs. Bryant, who was twenty-two years older than Ruth Ann and a very controlled woman, the act of sending over the gifts was really her expression of sympathy.

Finally, one day the doorbell rang and Mrs. Bryant stood at the door looking embarrassed, "I've been meaning to come, I tried to come a few times, but I'd end up driving around the block and then I'd drive home," she said. "I had no idea what to say to you." We both accepted how she felt, but her reaction brought out the reality of how uncomfortable so many people were with Johnny's condition.

I thought back to arriving in Tuscaloosa in 1958 and how I had been filled with good ideas about football and how I couldn't wait to share them with Coach Bryant. At one of our first meetings I couldn't believe that I was sitting in the same room with coaches like Jerry Claiborne and Pat James and that I was one of them. I remembered the day Coach Bryant asked us a question about how we'd have the fullbacks line up on a play where they were moving laterally. Nobody said anything for a while, so I finally spoke up and said, "Coach, I'd have them in a two-point stance."

Everybody looked at me for a while, and finally Coach Bryant said, "Well I can tell you one thing. We're sure not doing it that way." I rarely spoke to Coach Bryant about Johnny. Occasionally he would ask me how Ruth Ann was doing, but we mostly kept the conversation focused on our work. As with everything else, Ruth Ann and I wanted the Bryants' approval, and we felt as though we were letting them down. I don't think I said another word for the rest of the year.

That day after Mrs. Bryant left, Ruth Ann said to me, "I'll take care of our little girls and I'll take care of Johnny, but I'll never be happy again."

Ruth Ann and I had grown up going to church. God and church were very important parts of our lives, just as they had been in our parents' lives. But we began to think that though we had loved and worshiped God, look what had happened to us. I wasn't sure I wanted to believe in a God who was punishing me by giving me a disabled child. On Sundays, even though it was a struggle for us to go to church, we'd end up going and taking Johnny with us. We'd always loved music and singing, but when we'd hold Johnny in our arms and the singing would start, tears would roll down Ruth Ann's cheeks, she just couldn't sing. Then we began to discover that our church friends were very supportive and caring, different than our other friends were. After the service they would take the time to visit with us. Many of them would hold Johnny and ask the questions that we were longing to hear, questions like, "How is Johnny getting along with all those sisters? Is he sleeping? Is he rolling over yet?" Their concern meant a lot to us, and slowly we began to feel a little better about everything. Now, for the first time in months, coffee smelled good again, and the dull, aching pain in my head that I had tried to push away was beginning to disappear.

As the weeks slowly crept by, the characteristics of Down syndrome became even more pronounced in Johnny. But just as he was changing, so was I. I started not to care that his fingers were beginning to club and that his head was smaller than other babies'. When I picked him up and held him for a long time I felt a certain calmness. Unlike Anna Lee and Laurie, who had colic and, during their first years, woke up several times a night crying, Johnny was a docile, quiet little guy. I sensed that he needed me, but I was finding that I needed him, too. I felt a strong desire to protect him. When I'd get home from work I'd start giving him his bedtime bottle, which always took him a long time to drink. We'd sit there together quietly and I'd enjoy the peace. I found I was falling in love with my son, and I felt a strong desire to protect him.

All fall I had been distracted and unable to give my work the full attention that it needed. But slowly I was feeling happier and calmer and I found that I was able to relate to my players and the other coaches a little bit better than I had. We were having another winning season, just like the year before. As predicted, Joe Namath was emerging as a star, throwing three touchdown passes against Georgia in the opening game of the season.

One evening, when Johnny was four months old, just before a big game against Tennessee, I noticed that he was having difficulty breathing and his stomach looked distended. I quickly took the bottle out of his mouth and examined his little face. I thought maybe it had a bluish tint to it.

"Ruth Ann," I called. She came running up the stairs.

"Have you ever seen Johnny's face this color?" I asked.

She picked him up and looked at him. "We'd better call the doctor right away." She held him close to her and patted his back while I ran to the phone and called the doctor, but I got an answering service. We waited about ten minutes and called back again. This time my voice was more frantic and I told the service that we might have an emergency on our hands and that we had to speak to a doctor right away.

Minutes later the doctor called and told us to come right in. By this time it was 9 P.M. We lifted the girls up out of their beds and threw their coats over their pajamas as we climbed into the car and sped off to the doctor's office. The doctor examined him and said he had to be seen immediately by a cardiologist. "I'm sure he'll be all right until morning, but I suggest you get him there first thing," the doctor said as we left the office.

Once at the cardiologist's office we learned a bitter new truth — Johnny had a life-threatening heart defect. The doctor brought out a large chart of the heart and sat it on his desk as he walked us through the defect. "Johnny has a condition called Eisenmenger's syndrome." He pointed to a blue and pink section of the heart. "Essentially he has a hole in the wall of the heart which separates the heart chambers. The flow of blood between the heart and lungs meets with resistance. As Johnny gets older this resistance will increase. The oxygenated blood and the non-oxygenated blood get mixed up, and for the rest of his life he will have trouble getting enough oxygen." The doctor continued to point to the diagram of the chart and kept talking about left and right ventricles, atriums, and oxygenated blood, but it just wasn't sinking in. It was all unfamiliar territory to me, and I felt frustrated as he tried to communicate this critical information to us.

"The high pulmonary artery pressure in patients with Eisenmenger's syndrome causes increasing difficulty breathing, insufficient levels of oxygen in the blood, and swelling of lung tissue." The doctor looked sympathetically at Ruth Ann and me. I slumped in my seat, struggling to understand what he was saying, but only about a quarter of it made any sense.

The doctor then told us that 30 to 50 percent of children with Down syndrome have some kind of heart defect. Today most such defects are correctable by surgery. But in 1962 open-heart surgery just wasn't performed. Even if there had been a surgical procedure for Johnny he wouldn't have been able to tolerate anesthesia.

"Johnny should never be given anesthesia," the doctor said emphatically. I sat up in my chair as he continued. "His chances of surviving any kind of surgery are slim. It would be difficult for him to carry enough oxygen while he's in a sedated or sleep state. There would be the danger that he might not wake up."

I leaned back, clasped my hands together behind my head, and closed my eyes so tight that I saw stars. What would happen if Johnny had to have an appendectomy, a tonsillectomy, or, worse, if he was ever seriously injured? I asked the doctor what we would do, quietly praying that he would give me some kind of reassuring answer.

He shook his head and said solemnly, "We'll just have to cross that bridge if and when we get to it." I could see that the doctor felt sorry for us.

He recommended that Johnny take digitalis, a drug that slows the heart down. Years later, after successful surgical techniques were in place, Johnny developed pulmonary hypertension, a constriction in the arteries going from his heart to his lungs, which meant he could never be operated on. Johnny's heart was already weakened prematurely by the high pulmonary pressure needed to pass blood into his lungs. Eventually his lungs adjusted to the small amount of blood that was being funneled to them.

Now we were faced with a crisis that we had never expected. We had a baby who could die any minute. At times I wasn't sure if this was a blessing or a curse. Sometimes I thought if Johnny died this might be an honorable way out for me. I could say I'd done everything I could, but my son just didn't make it. I wouldn't have to travel through uncharted waters. If my child died as a baby, then I wouldn't have to experience the pain of worrying whether my daughters, when they became teenagers, would be embarrassed by their brother when their friends and dates came over to the house. Teenagers are upset with their parents about so many things anyway, maybe Johnny would just add to the problems. As a coach, my whole business was athletics and competition, and I was constantly surrounded by healthy, strong young men. As a father, it was tough to have a little boy and know that he would never be able to compete.

And then there was the worry that if he lived, who would take care of him if something happened to Ruth Ann and me? Here my children might be in their late forties and they'd have to care for a man around the same age! Would he be in the way? How would they possibly cope? How would their husbands feel? Would he ever have friends? Who would ever want him on their team? I just had no idea what Johnny would grow up to look like. Jack Horn's big face kept creeping into my mind. I saw him over and over again walking through the streets of Paris while my pals and I chased him and called him names.

Frantically, we went from one cardiologist to another and the message was always the same — be prepared, because Johnny probably will not live past the age of one. Ruth Ann started to take

Johnny's pulse to make sure she wasn't giving him too much digitalis, slowing his heart down so much that it would achieve just the opposite result from what we wanted. Some days she would take it twenty times a day. It would be 170 one day, 150 the next, and then 90. I'm not sure what that told us or what we could do about it. The tension was incredible: it felt like a sword over our heads that was ready to drop at any minute.

As the Christmas holidays of that first year approached we didn't feel like socializing. But there was the annual office party that I had to attend. Every other year Ruth Ann and the children had looked forward to the party. She always had fun dressing the girls up in their fanciest dresses and watching as they played with the other coaches' children and followed Santa Claus around, pulling on his belt, making sure he knew what they wanted for Christmas.

An assistant basketball coach at Alabama, Wimp Sanderson, and his wife, Annette, had a little boy, Scott, who was born two days after Johnny. We had never seen him and on this night they brought him to the office party. Scott, at six months, was a healthy baby with chubby pink cheeks and fat little legs. While the girls played with the other children, drank punch, and visited with Santa, Ruth Ann, Johnny, and I stayed in my office for a while, awkwardly trying to act as though we were deep in a private conversation. The secretaries and other coaches took turns holding Scott, fussing over him and passing him around. Finally, after hearing Scott's squeals and laughter, we came out of my office and Ruth Ann and I shook hands with Wimp and Annette and said the usual congratulatory things. Then one of the secretaries placed Scott in my arms. He laughed and babbled a little as I cradled him, and when I looked down at him, he reached up and tried to grab my nose. I quickly handed him back and I noticed that when the secretary put him in her chair he sat up — all by himself.

It was the first time I had held another baby since Johnny was born, and the differences between our two little boys was startling. Johnny was so much smaller and paler than Scott, and he had just started smiling. He couldn't sit up yet like Scott could, and when I held Johnny he felt limp and heavy in my arms. Now I looked closely at Johnny's eyes as he dozed off to sleep in Ruth Ann's arms and I thought how very slanted they looked, and how his skin was so light that it had an almost translucent quality to it.

Whenever I was around Wimp now it was hard for us to talk. I wanted to be happy for him, but all I could feel was a heaviness. Ruth Ann and Annette had always been good friends. But suddenly there was an awkwardness between them, too.

Our annual visit to Paris to see our parents for the holidays was coming up, and Ruth Ann and I dreaded making the trip. At six months old Johnny was fragile and weak. We were nervous about driving for ten hours from Tuscaloosa to Paris. On the other hand, we felt it was important for Anna Lee and Laurie to see Mammy and to spend time with my parents, who lived half a mile down the road from her, just like they did every holiday season. Maybe this would be the very last time that Johnny's grandparents would ever see him again. We still never discussed his problems in front of the girls, yet we knew times were difficult for them because we were so preoccupied. Finally we decided to go to Paris because we wanted them to have some normalcy in their lives.

Even though the population of Paris was then, and is still today, a sizable twenty-five thousand, it has always been more like a small town to Ruth Ann and me — like a village, really. In the mid 1940s, on Friday nights before a football game, cheerleaders led by the team band would march around our little square in the middle of town. Paris was very patriotic during World War II, and we would have savings bond rallies right on the square, where you could buy bonds. A fourth-grade classmate of mine, Janet Maples, had always claimed to be related to Gene Autry, and from time to time she'd show me pictures of him. Of course I doubted her, not really believing that she could possibly be related to such a famous person. But then one Saturday during a rally he rode into the middle of the town, dressed in his fringed and studded Cowboy outfit and riding his famous horse, Champion. We all sang along together as he serenaded us with his hit song "Back in the Saddle Again."

When we went to the picture shows on Saturday morning we would take along newspapers, coat hangers, and scrap iron. The metal was needed to make tanks and guns for the war effort. The picture shows at all of the five theaters in town — the Grand, the Plaza, the Main, the Lamar, and the Rex — were always free on Saturday morning if we brought in those materials.

To this day Paris has retained old-fashioned values. People still look out for each other. When folks go out of town they can count on their neighbors to turn the lights on in the house and take in the mail. Up until recently you could pick up a burger and shake at most local diners for under a dollar. The gas station attendants in town are still friendly and polite and call regulars by name. They even wash your windshield.

Almost all of our old friends and teachers from high school still lived there. Sometimes over the vacations Ruth Ann and I would go back to the C&C Drug Store, the place where we used to meet our friends in the evenings when we were in high school. We'd sit up at the soda fountain and inevitably we'd run into Hoot Gibson, my old basketball coach, and his wife, Jean, who had become a close friend of Ruth Ann's. Or Peter Barnett, our geometry teacher, who was also the beloved assistant football coach. Occasionally Coach Raymond Berry, the well-respected head football coach of Paris High, and the father of Ray Berry Jr., the great wide receiver and former head coach of the New England Patriots, would drop by to see if there were any players breaking curfew. We'd take up with these folks as if we still lived there. During the year we'd receive letters from our parents with the latest accounts of our friends' weddings, new babies, and job changes. I knew that many of them were following my career in sports.

We figured they'd all want to meet Johnny. We stayed with Mammy in her big old house on East Austin Street, right near the town square, down the street from my parents' house, and not far from the farm where she was born and raised. Sure enough, old friends did stop in to visit. I think most of them were surprised to find that our new baby, whom they'd heard was a mongoloid, was actually quite normal looking. As we watched our friends trying to be supportive and struggle to find the right words, it became obvious that they felt sorry for us. We felt little Christmas joy as they came and went from the house, and we also worried constantly about Johnny's health. In our minds we had disappointed the whole town of Paris.

When we returned home to Tuscaloosa, I started waking up every night just to check and make sure Johnny was breathing. Sometimes I would take his pulse and then I'd linger for a while. I'd sit down in the rocking chair in his room and simply stare at him as he slept. The gentle heaving up and down of his chest, the peaceful look on his little face, his tiny hands and feet all mesmerized me. I'd make up little songs with his name in them and I'd sing to him. Some nights I'd wind up his music box, pick him up, and rock him in the dark to the tune of "The Farmer in the Dell." With my ear up against his chest, I'd listen carefully for his heartbeat. Only then could I fall back asleep. I couldn't stop thinking about Johnny's health, and now more than anything in the world I wanted him to make it to his first birthday.

That spring as Johnny's first birthday approached he was starting to make little sounds and the peach fuzz on top of his head was changing into platinum blond hair. He was still tiny and delicate, but he had started to sit up and he was laughing a lot. When Ruth Ann would talk about the details of planning a birthday party for him, I'd quickly change the subject. I was so afraid that he wouldn't make it.

During the Memorial Day parade in Tuscaloosa, I looked over at Johnny sitting in his stroller amid a crowd of people and I watched him giggle and point at the different marching bands. When the antique fire trucks made their way slowly down the street and he clapped his little hands together, just like any other little boy, I thought: he's going to make it. That evening Ruth Ann sent out the invitations to his birthday party.

A couple of weeks later, when his first birthday arrived, there wasn't a cloud in the sky and Ruth Ann orchestrated the perfect backyard birthday celebration for Johnny. She set up little tables in the backyard and tied different-colored helium balloons on all the trees and baked a cake in the shape of a football. Johnny seemed to laugh the whole day as he smeared chocolate icing all over himself and some of the guests. We all watched, amazed, as he huffed and puffed and finally blew out the big blue candle on his cake. We sang "Happy Birthday" over and over that day, and even after the guests went home.

In the middle of the 1963 football season, right after we lost 10–6 to Florida, which was to be Alabama's last loss in Tuscaloosa for twenty years, we found out that Ruth Ann was pregnant again. As she began to show more I kept hoping that the baby would be a boy, and she did, too. But as her pregnancy progressed we were also becoming increasingly nervous that the child might not be healthy. Most mothers giving birth at Ruth Ann's age of twenty-nine had approximately a one in 950 chance of having a child with Down syndrome. But because she had already had one child with Down's she was at a much greater risk. The odds of having another child with Down's were now a startling one in one hundred. We also wanted Johnny to live to meet his new sibling, but the doctors were cautioning us that Johnny might not live to see his second birthday.

Like Johnny, Jacklyn Stallings was born one month prematurely, on April 28, 1964, just a little over a month away from Johnny's second birthday. When the doctor came into the waiting room on that warm spring afternoon and told me that she was a healthy normal baby, I let out an audible sigh of relief and sank back into my chair. I guess I couldn't believe it. The last nine months had been stressful, worrying daily whether the baby would be all right. We were only momentarily disappointed that we didn't have a baby boy because we were so thrilled that Jackie didn't have any problems. I thought how when the first two children were born we took it for granted that they would be healthy, something we could never be sure of again.

When Johnny turned two, we didn't even have a party for him because we were so busy with four children. With Anna Lee, seven, Laurie, five, Johnny, and a newborn, we had so much to do that at times we were a little less obsessed with Johnny's health. After all, I kept telling myself, he had made it this far. But just as we'd start to relax a little, the doctors would warn us that he might only have one more year to live at the most. We felt the threat of losing him keenly and began to change the way we lived.

Football coaches as a rule tend to live for the next game, the next season, and the season after that. There have been plenty of times when we've played a game and thirty seconds after it was over, I've started to think about the next week's game. And after the end of that season, there would always be next year. Now I was slowing down, taking my time a little more with my family, my friends, and my work. I wasn't concentrating on the future so much, because I didn't know from one day to the next if my son was going to live or not.

CHAPTER 3

▼

COLLEGE STATION

ONE Sunday night in December of 1964, the telephone rang just as we were all leaving the house to go to church. I stopped outside the door and ran back inside. "We're going to be late, Bebes," Ruth Ann called to me as she piled the children into our brand-new Chrysler. But I kept going. Something made me want to answer that telephone.

A friendly voice on the other end of the line said, "Coach Stallings? This is Pete Peterson. I'm a member of the board of trustees at Texas A&M." For a minute I thought he was going to ask for a donation to the alumni fund, but then he said, "We've been watching the Tide win and hearing about the great job you're doing over there, and we wondered if you would be interested in coming to College Station and interviewing for the job here as head coach."

Head coach! Texas A&M! I swallowed and pulled at my ear. I wasn't sure if I was hearing him correctly. "We'll send a private plane for you early tomorrow morning, if you're interested," he said.

This was a dream job. It was a position I thought I wouldn't have a shot at for at least five or ten more years. I have no idea what I said next on the phone, all I know is that early the following morning I was in my car, headed four miles out to the airport in Tuscaloosa. I drove past the historic brick buildings along the Quad, slowing down at the Denny Chimes, the tall big brick monument, where every year football captains make a ritual of leaving their handprints in wet cement, and I imagined myself leaving Tuscaloosa behind and being back at A&M, this time as head coach. Just eleven years earlier, as a freshman there, I had been one of the skinniest kids on the team, weighing in at only 160 pounds. Bobby Drake Keith, then my roommate and now an assistant coach at the University of Oklahoma, wasn't known for being very big, but he weighed a full twenty-five pounds more than I did.

Every night before I went to bed, I weighed myself without fail, carefully recording my weight on a chart, hoping that the number would increase by morning. I'd eat two or three portions at dinner, finishing up with as many desserts as I could fit on my plate while Bobby and my other classmates watched me in disbelief. I'd even spend an hour each day lifting weights. But no matter how hard I tried, I couldn't gain a pound. In fact, I had to sew sheepskin into the lining of my football pants so that my knees wouldn't bruise. I never thought of myself as a great player, I didn't think I was especially strong or fast, but I was sure passionate about the game and willing to give it everything I had.

When the news came out in February of 1954 that the new A&M football coach was going to be Bear Bryant, I went around campus asking my friends, "Have any of you ever heard of Bear Bryant?" I had no idea who he was because I only knew what was going on in the Southwest Conference.

Coach Bryant had been the head coach at the University of Kentucky, which was in the Southeastern Conference, for the last eight years. Until they hired him from the University of Maryland, Kentucky had never won a championship, never had a bowl team, never even had a winning team, for that matter. But he soon turned all that around and started winning ball games, putting the team on the map and making a name for himself, too. But Kentucky was primarily a basketball school. Coach Bryant liked to be number one wherever he was, and he began to view the basketball coach, the famed Adolph Rupp, as a rival. After it looked like Rupp wasn't going to retire anytime soon, Coach Bryant became more and more frustrated and decided that it was time to make a change, except Kentucky wouldn't let him out of his contract. Why would they want to part with such a winner? Finally, it took the governor of Kentucky to release him. Of course, he had his sights set on a job at Alabama, his alma mater, or Arkansas, in his home state, but there were no openings at those schools. A&M, though, was looking for a winning coach who would turn around a losing team.

When Coach Bryant arrived in College Station that winter, replacing Coach Ray George, he was introduced to the majority of the student body — over six thousand of us. We were suited up in our uniforms, waiting for him at the Grove, the outdoor theater where all the yell practices and rallies have always taken place at A&M. My friends and I hurried to the front of the stage to get a look at our new coach. I couldn't get over what a towering figure he was, standing tall at six feet four inches and probably weighing close to two hundred pounds. He was ruggedly handsome, too — with a full head of brown wavy hair and piercing blue eyes.

He walked out onstage, whipped off his coat, threw it to the ground, stomped on it, and then rolled up the sleeves of his white shirt. He yelled into the microphone, his deep voice booming, "We're going to win, folks." We all went wild and started hollering. We kept up like that for at least five minutes until he quieted us down. I knew right then and there that if Coach Bryant said we were going to win, then we would. Never mind that we had lost our last five games in the fall of 1953 by a combined score of 133–41. Coach Bryant had this kind of powerful, commanding presence and you believed every word he said.

A few weeks after he arrived, he led us through an excruciatingly tough spring training. All throughout the practices I kept thinking how much I wanted to gain weight. I knew that if I were heavier I'd be a much better player. One afternoon after practice, Coach Bryant pulled me aside. "Bebes," he said, "you tell me you've tried everything to gain weight. What do you think the problem is?"

I hesitated, a little embarrassed, and then I tried to think of some reason why I couldn't put on weight. "Ever since I was a baby, I've had trouble in my right ear because of infections," I said.

"Well, maybe you should see about an operation on that ear," he said. "I'll bet the infection is draining into your system and that's why you're not gaining."

During spring break I decided to go to Baylor Hospital in Dallas and have an operation called a mastoidectomy on my ear. Our team doctor told me that Baylor had an excellent ear, nose, and throat doctor. I stayed in the hospital a few nights and my parents came and visited me. But after a couple of days they had to go back home to their jobs. They gave me some money to ride the bus the 180 miles back to College Station. But instead I hitchhiked back to school.

As soon as I was discharged from the hospital, I went out onto the highway, my head all bandaged up, and I got dizzy and sick while I was hitchhiking. I sat on my suitcase and waited until a guy picked me up, and then I slept the entire time in the backseat of his car. He delivered me right to the athletic dorm.

At a meeting one night in late August of 1954 Coach Bryant told the team of about one hundred players that we should each get a blanket, a pillow, and a couple changes of clothing because we were going on a little trip. We had absolutely no idea where we were going or what was going to happen as we boarded two buses and headed out to an arid part of the desolate hill country in West Texas called Junction, a couple hundred miles from campus. I later heard Coach Bryant refer to our destination as "a flyspeck on the map out in the hill country near Kerrville." It was the place where A&M geology and engineering students spent the summer doing field-work. When we arrived I could see that there were absolutely no facilities for football. The geology students lived in sorry-looking Quonset huts — one-room structures with corrugated tin roofs, concrete floors, and screened-in sides — which we were assigned to sleep in. There were six double bunks in each hut and a small bathroom to one side.

When we first got there it was like summer camp. We found a pretty little swimming hole nearby where we idled away the afternoons after playing touch football all morning. But a couple of days later everything changed. Just before sunrise on September 1, 1954, a date I'll never forget, the manager, Troy Summerlin, came roaring through the barracks blowing a whistle, yelling at the top of his lungs for everyone to wake up, get out of bed, put on their uniform, and be out on the field in five minutes. I wasn't sure if I was dreaming or not as I jumped out of my bunk, grabbed my pants and jersey, and pulled them on. Even though it was still dark out, we were all lined up, fully dressed, and out on the field a few minutes later. Then as the sun came up over the mountain Coach Bryant came out of his Quonset hut and we started up without eating a bit of breakfast.

West Texas was in the middle of a drought and nothing was growing. Trees that should have been green were brown. It was windy and dusty and by ten o'clock in the morning the temperature had climbed to one hundred degrees. The field didn't have much grass — it was mostly gravel — and my hands quickly became bloodied and scarred by the rocks and large sandburs, which we called goatheads. At night, I'd be sound asleep just as my head hit the pillow. We went through two-hour full-contact practices in the mornings. Then we would break for breakfast, meetings, then two more hours of practice. Then we'd have lunch, a little rest, and we'd practice again and have drills like one-on-ones, force drills, tackling drills, and dash to dash — anything to perfect our technique.

We practiced every day, even on Sundays before church, and only broke to eat, have meetings, and rest. There was no time for fun or opportunities just to sit around and relax. Then when the Southwest Conference press tours (a group of twenty or so journalists who would travel across the state from university to university to speak with players and coaches for their upcoming stories) came out to Junction, we had to practice two hours before conducting interviews, and then we practiced two hours afterward.

All the underclassmen got last choice on where to sleep, so I was stuck in a top bunk. In between practices we'd go lie down for a little while. But I'd be lying there in the middle of the day, and my face would be about a foot away from the hot tin roof. I could barely breathe, it was so sweltering.

A lot of the players quit and left in the middle of the night, hitchhiking back to A&M. Others would wait by the water fountain after lunch. You'd see a player there and you knew that he was trying to get up the courage to tell Coach Bryant he was going to quit. At least if you told Coach Bryant you were quitting he paid for your bus ticket back to school. But those of us who stuck it out ended up staying in Junction for ten days, ten of the longest days in my life. I wished a thousand times that we would leave the place, but quitting football simply was not an option. It is now history that we went to Junction in two buses and returned to the campus in one, and that bus was about half full, with only twenty-nine players on board. It was much more demanding than boot camp,

49

but going through such a difficult training period brought us all closer together, and we ended up respecting Coach Bryant's excellent coaching staff — guys like Jerry Claiborne, who later became the coach and athletic director at Kentucky and at Maryland; Phil Cutchin, who went on to become head coach of Oklahoma State; and Elmer Smith, who would later work as my assistant. We knew when we left Junction that we were capable of being winners.

School officials and the news media started criticizing Coach Bryant's tactics. But what they didn't understand was that he had to find out who really wanted to play, and toughness was what he looked for in a player. Under the old regime those qualities had not been important. Coach Bryant knew how to take an average player, toughen him up, and make sure he was superbly conditioned, so that he could play well in the fourth quarter. That's how he would win games.

Our first game, against Texas Tech, I was not a starter, but things were going so miserably that Coach Bryant put me in the game early in the third quarter. Even though we lost badly (the score was 41–9), I guess I had some good tackles and some decent plays, and the following Monday Coach Bryant gathered the team together. He gave us all one of his intense looks and lectured us on how we could improve. And then, with the whole team present, he looked over at me and said, "My biggest mistake was not playing that skinny kid over there enough." What an incredibly proud moment that was in my life. Obviously, though, the operation on my ear hadn't affected my weight.

We had a terrible 1–9 season Coach Bryant's first year. I don't think that he had any idea that we'd lose as many players as we did at Junction. Who knows what the outcome for the season would have been if they had stayed? But two years later, in 1956, the players voted me a tricaptain along with Jack Pardee and Lloyd Hale, and we enjoyed a 9–0–1 record that year, which was also our first conference title in sixteen seasons. I'm convinced that our trip to Junction ultimately helped Coach Bryant to unify our team.

Now, as I drove to the airport terminal, I became more and more excited about the prospect of going back to College Station and becoming the head coach of A&M, and of being able to make a difference in the players' lives, just the way Coach Bryant had influenced me as a young player. Hank Foldberg, Coach Bryant's successor in 1959, had just been fired as head coach because under his tenure A&M had won a total of only eighteen games and had lost forty-seven. The program badly needed to be turned around. The school was longing for Coach Bryant's winning ways. I was twenty-nine years old, optimistic and a little cocky.

Now here I was interviewing for a position that, if I got it, meant that I was going to be the youngest coach in major college football at that time. A heady thought. I was certain that I could accomplish great things.

Tony Hildenfels, a member of the A&M board of trustees, sent his eight-seater Aero-Commander to greet me at the small airport. The pilot took my overnight bag and led me to the plane. I felt like royalty as I climbed the stairs and entered the small, luxurious cabin. After a two-and-a-half-hour flight, we landed at the little Esterwood Airport, which was practically next door to the A&M campus. As I drove through College Station I noticed it didn't look a whole lot different than it had when I left. The small downtown was still the center of the action, there were no shopping centers, and the tallest building in town was still only three stories tall. The train, which headed southbound for Houston and northbound for Dallas, ran right through the middle of town, just like it always had. But when I was a student at A&M there had been an area of about five miles that somewhat divided the towns of College Station and Bryan. Now that area was more built up with houses and the two places were more or less joined together to form one big town. It was hard to tell when you were leaving College Station and passing into Bryan.

I guess to some young people A&M had all the attraction of a reformatory in 1964. Located seventy miles northwest of Houston, in east central Texas, there was little to do but study and play football. I've even heard the college referred to as Sing Sing on the Brazos (River). But I never thought much about being isolated when I attended college. All I knew was that you could still get the best education in the world at A&M and you could learn to have pride in something, whether it was the corps, the band, or the life of the football team. I became an enthusiastic "Aggie," as A&M students are called, because of the tremendous spirit that I found on the campus.

Founded in 1876, A&M was the only school in the Southwest Conference still without coeds, a fact that pleased Ruth Ann. The student body had increased slightly from about seven thousand students to eight thousand. But when I went to school there it was all military — we called it the Cadet Corps. There was an Air Force ROTC and an Army ROTC, so you were either in a squadron or a company. The seniors were the ranking officers and freshmen had no rank. The athletes lived in a place called Hart Hall. We had to fall out in the morning and march to breakfast. In fact, the Cadet Corps would march to all of their meals.

Now, years later, the athletes had moved into Henderson Hall, a dorm named for a great A&M player, "Jitterbug" Henderson. After Coach Bryant came along he slowly changed things to give the athletes a little bit of a break, so eventually we didn't have to take the time to put on full uniforms, make formations, and march to chow.

As I sat around an oval-shaped mahogany table, listening carefully as each trustee interviewed me at the house on campus that housed the board of trustees, I was surprised that their questions were so short and direct. It seemed they had already made up their minds to hire me, and it occurred to me that maybe Coach Bryant had put in a good word on my behalf. Sure enough, right then and there I was offered the job. And just as quickly, I agreed to accept it. We hadn't even discussed money.

There was a great deal of prestige and visibility in being head coach of A&M. I just couldn't believe that I might have a similar kind of recognition as Coach Darrell Royal, the coach of the University of Texas, who was better known than the governor of Texas. I was nervous and thrilled all at once, and I found myself telling the board that I had no doubt we'd win the Southwest Conference championship in three years or they could have the job back. Never mind that A&M was coming off a 1–9 season and hadn't won a championship in ten years! I was walking on a cloud when I left that meeting.

As the plane headed back to Alabama, I was filled with excitement. But after two tumultuous years in Tuscaloosa, I also had some serious doubts about moving Johnny from our friends and our safe environment there. I sat staring out of the window, trying to sort through the last twenty-four hours. I had four young children at home, one who had a severe heart problem and needed constant attention. Ruth Ann and I were just starting to feel more relaxed about Johnny's disabilities when we were around our friends, who were beginning to know him. They were asking us about him more, and I noticed that the more some of these folks saw him, the more they smiled at him and treated him like any other child. We had spent a great deal of time searching for ways to make other people feel more comfortable with Johnny, going out of our way to reassure anyone who seemed scared or awkward around him. Ruth Ann often invited the neighbor children over, and she'd sit there and play their games with them for a while until they finally included Johnny and she knew they wouldn't tease or hurt him. We were just beginning to loosen up a little on that score.

Yet not a day would go by when we wouldn't worry whether

our son was going to live. I was still waking up in the middle of every night, going into his room, and making sure that his little heart was beating. And Ruth Ann never missed a day of checking Johnny's pulse. She often made the hourlong drive to Birmingham to the cardiologist's office. We now trusted and respected Johnny's doctors and had finally built up a close relationship with them.

I glanced out the window as we approached our landing. I felt as if I were caught in a whirlwind. Pete Peterson had called me only late yesterday afternoon. A lot had happened, too fast.

When I arrived home I burst in the door, tossed my overnight bag in the hallway, and told Ruth Ann about the job offer and how I had accepted. She threw her arms around me and said, "Oh, Bebes, how wonderful!" Seeing her so excited made me temporarily forget any of my concerns, and I picked her up and twirled her in the air. I ran outside to where the children were playing and gave each one of them a whirl, too. But when I held Johnny high and looked up at him, I grew quieter. After a while, I left the children in the backyard, went back into the house, and sat down on the sofa.

"What is it, Bebes?" Ruth Ann came over and sat down next to me. I immediately began to express my reservations about moving our family all the way to College Station, but she wouldn't listen.

"This is an opportunity of a lifetime. We've got to go for it," she said. I'm sure deep down she shared some of my worries, but she never told me.

The board of trustees wanted me to start the very next week. Alabama had finished a winning season and was headed for the Orange Bowl, but I couldn't go because I had to hire a staff at A&M and start recruiting. I wanted to tell Coach Bryant about my new position right away, before he read about it in the newspapers or saw it announced on the television news. That night I called him at his hotel. He was in New York with his friend, Julian Lackey, on business. I thought that he'd be as tickled as I was about my job offer.

"Coach Bryant, this is Bebes. I just wanted to call and tell you they've offered me a job as head coach at A&M and I've accepted it." There was silence on the other end of the phone. "You know, I've always appreciated the opportunity you gave me coaching in college and getting me started at Alabama. I have really enjoyed working for the very best and I just want to thank you."

After I hung up, I was a little confused by how quiet Coach Bryant had been while I was talking to him. A few days later I ran into Julian, who told me that Coach Bryant had started to cry when I told him that I was leaving. Coach Bryant had looked over at Julian and said, "I've just lost one of my coaches." Julian tried to comfort Coach Bryant, presuming that meant his assistant had died! He had just named me his assistant head coach at Alabama, and I knew that he was sad and somewhat disappointed that I was leaving.

As the last few days in Tuscaloosa approached I felt more and more excited about my new job, but it was also difficult to leave. I wanted to go around and say goodbye to all of the people in the office who had meant so much to me — fellow assistants like Jerry Claiborne, Clem Gryska, Sam Bailey, Ken Meyer, and Dee Powell, who had quietly supported me during the last two difficult years with Johnny. As I said my goodbyes I realized that each in his own way had shown me that he cared about my son and that they, too, were rooting for him.

Finally I came to Coach Bryant's office. As he motioned for me to come in, he stood up, put his hand on my shoulder, and said, "Bebes, I'm going to give you three pieces of advice: Don't look back. Don't lose your guts. And go out on that field and make something happen." I promised him that I would keep in touch.

Mrs. Bryant had a goodbye tea for Ruth Ann at her house. She asked Anna Lee and Laurie to come and open the door for the guests who came to wish our family well. The girls, dressed in their full-skirted Sunday dresses, were so proud to be included. Ruth Ann believes that Mrs. Bryant was trying to make amends for not having been more supportive when Johnny was born.

I flew right back to College Station and lived in the Memorial Student Center on campus until Ruth Ann and the children could come. Meanwhile she had pressure to do a lot in a short amount of time. The house had to be sold and she had to get four young children, three cats, and all of our possessions packed. I worried constantly about how Johnny would make such a grueling trip. But a month and a half later, after Alabama won the 1964 national championship, Ruth Ann drove the family over six hundred miles nonstop and arrived in College Station.

We rented a small ranch house looking out on a little creek in Bryan and talked about building a home once we got more settled. Almost immediately we invited Pete Peterson and his wife, Olida, over for dessert and coffee. We still had cartons and boxes stacked three and four high in the hallway of our small ranch house, our curtains weren't hung up, and we'd barely unpacked our suitcases. We didn't even know where our toothbrushes were. But we wanted to get to know the Petersons. It was important that they like and accept us. As a trustee, he was one of my bosses and one of the key people responsible for hiring me.

Ruth Ann spent the day baking pies and searching through boxes for our best china and silver to set the table with. When I came home we dressed the children up in their nicest clothes. Our three girls had on matching flowered dresses and black patent leather shoes and had pink bows in their hair. Johnny wore a little one-piece shorts outfit just like the ones we so often saw John John Kennedy wearing. John John was just one year older than Johnny and his picture was in national newspapers and magazines all the time. The nation was still reeling from the shock of President Kennedy's assassination the previous fall and John John, an adorable little boy, had become a symbol of American courage. We even cut

Johnny's platinum blond hair in a bowl-like cut similar to John John's. Right before the guests arrived we brushed his hair until it shined. We clipped his coarse little fingernails, which were discolored because his heart condition prevented enough oxygen from reaching his extremities, and we polished his saddle shoes. Johnny looked like a handsome little prince.

There was no doubt about it, we wanted to make a good impression. Of course, we always spent a lot of time dressing Johnny up. We never would have admitted it then, but we thought Johnny might be more accepted if he looked cute.

When the Petersons walked in, the children were outside in the backyard playing and we called them to come and meet our guests. Laurie and Anna Lee came running up the back steps and then Jackie, who had just started taking a few steps, climbed each stair slowly, holding on to the banister. Her little dress was too long and she kept getting tangled up in it as she teetered to the top of the steps. Pete and Olida smiled as they watched her climb the stairs and applauded loudly as she reached the top.

Last came Johnny. He couldn't walk, but he had a swift, awkward crawl that was really scooting on his hips while sitting. He looked like a little crab as he awkwardly propelled his body by putting his arms and chest on the step above his legs and hoisting up his lower body. By the time he reached the top his outfit was filthy, as were his hands and knees. He inched over to me and squeezed my legs and I picked him up and put him on my shoulders. The Petersons studied him for a few seconds. Then they both grimaced and quickly turned away, focusing their attentions on the girls — especially Jackie. She was a cute, outgoing nine-month-old with curly dark hair and an infectious grin.

As we sat down and ate dessert Johnny crawled around messing the house up like any two-and-a-half-year-old child would do. He couldn't talk except for saying an unintelligible "mama" and "pop,

pop," and on this night he seemed especially frustrated and screamed a high, piercing wail whenever he wanted something. Ruth Ann carried Johnny over to the sink, trying to wash the dirt off of him, but he wouldn't let her and he screamed and cried until she stopped trying. Olida and Pete looked more and more uncomfortable and continued to focus on Jackie, remarking how adorable she was. Ruth Ann kept getting up from the table to offer everybody more coffee and pie while I tried to keep the conversation flowing. Finally she felt that everyone was so ill at ease that she put Johnny to bed.

We tried to resume our visiting, but none of us could think of much to say beyond the talk of A&M football. We knew that they knew that Johnny wasn't "normal" and they could tell that we knew how uncomfortable they were, but no one said anything about Johnny. After a long awkward silence, Olida and Pete announced they had to leave. The perfect evening we had envisioned ended in a disappointment.

After the Petersons walked out the door, Ruth Ann and I didn't even do the dishes. Instead, we headed straight for bed. "Do you think people will ever accept Johnny here?" she asked me as we got ready for bed. I had a hard time answering her because I felt just as troubled over the evening. On the one hand, I wanted the Petersons to like us, but they hadn't been receptive to Johnny and I was deeply hurt and angry.

"I'm sure things will get better," I finally answered, but I wasn't so sure. I didn't sleep for the rest of the night, worrying about having to start over again in a new environment. Ruth Ann became preoccupied with thoughts of whether we would ever be fully accepted in College Station because of Johnny. I never would have admitted to those feelings before then, but after that night I had them too.

The next day I went off to the office early, once again pouring myself into my work. I felt bad about leaving Ruth Ann to stay home with the four children every day. While I could immerse myself in my job and enjoy a staff of secretaries, equipment people, and assistants working for me, she had to deal with the uncertainty and chaos of raising children by herself with little help. She was busy enrolling Anna Lee in first grade, helping her adjust to a new school, taking Laurie to morning kindergarten, picking her up, meeting and getting to know the staff and coaches' wives, and settling into a different house. And, at two and a half, Johnny still had to be carried everywhere. All day long she had to encounter people and prove to them that Johnny was a lovable little boy. There was no escape for her, as there was for me. When I got home at night she usually told me only about the good things that had happened with the children. But I knew what a tough time she was having and that she was being scrutinized as the new football coach's wife, maybe doubly so because of Johnny.

That winter I'd been traveling a lot, hitting the recruiting trail pretty hard from December through February, and I'd signed up sixty-two players. The pressure was on and it seemed as though the whole world was looking at me, the new young coach, expecting a miracle. My team was to be headed up by a group of seniors who had won only three games in their college careers. My first season looked like it was going to be challenging, to say the least.

One of the first things I did at work was to call in Elmer Smith and give him the job of assistant head coach. In a very short time he went from getting fired along with A&M head coach Hank Fold-berg and most of his staff to becoming my offensive line coach. At fifty-nine years old, he was a seasoned coach who had had a lot of success as a head coach at a small college in Arkansas. I had developed great respect for Elmer when he coached me during the Junction trip. He was a hard-nosed man with a lot of common sense who was one of the few coaches to rest the regulars the week after a tough Saturday game if he thought they needed a break. I knew Elmer would be an excellent addition to my staff, kind of an elder statesman, because the other coaches I'd hired — including my teammates from A&M like Dee Powell, Don Watson, and Lloyd Taylor — were roughly my age. But I had no idea then what Elmer would eventually mean to our family.

Elmer was a striking figure as he walked out onto the football field; his signature brown felt hat always tipped to one side, and his big baggy shirts and pants flapped in the wind. The players became real serious when they saw Elmer coming their way. He'd rest one of his enormous hands on a player's shoulder and you could just about hear a pin drop out on the field.

Late one spring afternoon I sat in my office fielding phone calls and trying to catch up on paperwork. Elmer appeared in the doorway. "Got a minute?" he asked.

"Come on in," I said, offering him a chair and a Coke.

Elmer sat down and cleared his throat, "I've heard a little about your boy, Bebes, and I wondered if I could go over to your house sometime and pay him a visit."

I was surprised by Elmer's offer, and at first I thought he was just being polite to his boss, or trying to make small talk. But when he pinned me down to a date — the next Saturday, right after football practice — I was deeply touched that he had extended himself in this way. As Saturday rolled around I wondered if Elmer would forget our date. But right after practice there he was by my side, reminding me that he was coming over to visit with Johnny.

Johnny took to Elmer the first time they met. Elmer didn't even have time to take his jacket and hat off before Johnny was trying to get his attention by showing him his trucks and blocks. Elmer got right down on the floor with him and the two sat there cross-legged for an hour as they played "crash the trucks" and built a castle out of wooden blocks. At one point Elmer bent his head down and

Johnny grabbed his brown felt hat and put it on top of his own head. It covered most of his face and Elmer carried Johnny over to a mirror and tipped the hat back so he could get a better look at himself. They both laughed, and then Elmer grabbed the hat back and Johnny tried to get it back from him. They kept up a playful tug-of-war for a good twenty minutes — I'm sure it was fifteen minutes longer than Elmer would have wished, but he acted like he was having a wonderful time with Johnny.

I noticed that Elmer looked Johnny in the eye and really talked to him when they played together. He'd chatter about the football team, the weather, his car — it didn't seem to matter that Johnny rarely responded. Johnny tried to talk and answer back, but nobody could really understand him. Elmer made a point of visiting Johnny once every two weeks, and he usually brought along a little toy of some sort that he knew he would like. He'd take him for a ride around our neighborhood in his green Chrysler convertible and, to the neighbors' chagrin, let him honk the horn as often and as loud as he wanted. Eventually he taught Johnny to say his name. Johnny would follow Elmer around the yard shouting, "Emer! Emer!" I think "Emer" was one of Johnny's first words.

I watched as this enormous man would pick up my fragile little boy, swing him around, and lift him up on his shoulders, and my heart would soar. No one outside our family had ever given Johnny this much love and attention. Elmer talked about Johnny around the office and occasionally I'd hear him telling some of the other coaches about a cute thing Johnny had done. Some time later one of my coaches told me that Elmer had a brother who had Down syndrome.

Most nights when I'd return home from the office I'd find the children out on the patio. "Walk, Johnny, walk!" I'd hear the big girls shouting as I came around to the back from the driveway. Anna Lee would be standing on one side of the fifteen-foot stretch of flagstone and Laurie would be on the other. In between the girls would stand Jackie, Johnny, and General, our new German shepherd puppy. Jackie would take the small, uneven steps of a one-year-old and navigate her way toward one of her sisters. Anna Lee and Laurie would be coaxing Johnny to follow her. Then one of them would hold on to his hands and try to get his unsteady, wobbly little legs, which appeared to have all the strength of wet noodles, to touch the pavement. General followed along, yipping the whole time, nipping at Johnny's heels and wagging his tail. Johnny's legs simply had no power, and at two and a half, he had just started to push up and stand — as the girls had before they were a year old.

Johnny wanted to do the things that Jackie, who was two years younger, could do. Whenever Jackie learned something new — like eating with a spoon or drinking from a cup, Johnny would be interested in trying, too. He was always behind her, always trying to catch up. He wasn't competing with her, he just didn't have that kind of temperament. But you could see Johnny watching Jackie, mimicking her. He loved her and was fascinated by her good nature, her sense of adventure, and all of the things that she could show him how to do.

In my own backyard I could see that my girls had a common goal — they were banding together to get their brother to walk. Night after night, as I watched my children perform this ritual I realized that this was just the kind of teamwork I wanted to see from my players every day. It was my job to get my whole team — defensive linemen like Billy Hobbs and receiver Tommy Maxwell and Edd Hargett, our quarterback — to work together as if they were on one heartbeat. In fact, the girls were so intent on getting Johnny to walk that they needed coaxing to come in the house and sit down to dinner.

Laurie and Anna Lee thought Johnny couldn't walk because he had a heart condition. They still didn't know that he had Down syndrome. They hadn't yet mentioned to us that Johnny looked a little different. But as they kept working with him they began to ask us questions. "Why do we always have to be so careful with Johnny?" Anna Lee asked us one day.

It was time to tell them that Johnny had Down syndrome. We sat the children down on the sofa in the living room and tried to explain that their brother would always look different and that he would have delays in many of the things that he tried to do. "He might not ever be able to do a lot of the things that you do easily," said Ruth Ann. The girls sat there, fidgeting, and I wasn't really sure how much they understood. Pretty soon they asked if they could go outside and play. Later that afternoon I thought how it didn't really matter to them that Johnny was different. He was simply their beautiful brother.

Still, I worried constantly that they were getting too attached to a sibling who could die at any time. After a few months as I watched my daughters continue to try to get Johnny to walk without any progress, and then fail, I'd think how disappointed they'd be if their brother never ever learned to walk. We knew so little about children with Down syndrome that in my mind I seriously doubted that he could ever learn to walk or do much of anything.

Most of the time we didn't plan for Johnny's future, and we never prodded him to do the things that we had pushed our girls to do. We didn't try to get him to achieve many physical goals because we were scared that he was too weak. But the girls did. I'm sure it was because they saw their friends' baby sisters and brothers accomplishing things. Ruth Ann and I longed for someone to guide us, to give us some idea of what to expect from this child. What would the next year be like? The next month or the next day? There was simply no one — no doctor or friend — to tell us what Johnny could and couldn't do.

When Johnny was running a temperature or when he had an

earache or sore throat the whole family became frustrated because he couldn't communicate what the problem was. I felt a deep sorrow because my son and I couldn't talk. I often wondered if he'd ever be able to climb up on my lap and read a book with me the way that I did with the girls, or if he'd ever be able to tell me how his day at school was, or if he felt afraid or sad.

At two and a half, instead of talking Johnny would make sounds that were often so loud and uncontrollably shrill that you'd just want to cover your ears and run away. He wanted you to understand and give him some feedback, but eventually he'd just give up. He'd crawl into another room, shut the door, and be by himself.

I remembered back to the time when Laurie was first learning to talk. She had been about thirteen months old and we were in our backyard in Tuscaloosa. "Pwiddy fwowers," she said as she pulled up several dandelions from the ground. Ruth Ann and I were so proud, and we continued to be thrilled as she became a real talker that year. I doubted I would ever have an experience like that with my son.

Johnny's potty training seemed to take forever and he had trouble with simple tasks like drinking from a cup. He would take his diaper off sometimes and run around, having accidents in the house. You could tell he was embarrassed because he would go and hide when we would be cleaning up after him. Many nights I'd sit in front of his high chair and hold a cup while he tried to drink from it, but often he'd choke and I'd have to stop. He wanted to talk, and he wanted to walk. You could see it on his face. He would get a determined look, bite his little lip, and you could feel how badly he wanted to learn. But he had to try twice as hard as the girls did to accomplish anything.

During the day, when I would be out on the field with the team during practices and see one of my players who had a lot of talent but wasn't using it, I'd get upset and lose my patience. All day long

I'd be surrounded by players who were blessed with strong bodies and who were natural athletes, and then I'd come home and find Johnny trying to maneuver himself across a room or struggling just to make himself understood by Ruth Ann and me and his sisters. And I'd think how much I'd like to see him have just a fraction of that ability of my players.

I had always been a big Yankees fan while I was growing up because they beat just about everybody they ever played. Yankees pennants covered my bedroom walls, and my friends and I traded baseball cards of players like Mel Ott, Joe DiMaggio, Ted Williams, and Bob Feller. I would sit in the living room and listen to every game on the radio, trying to predict when Mel Allen, the famous baseball announcer who hailed from Alabama and was a classmate of Coach Bryant's at the university, would declare, "How about that!" Then after a batter would hit a home run I'd wait for his familiar "Going, going, gone!" All of my pals gathered around the radio at my house to listen to the World Series games in the 1940s — first in 1941, then '42, '43, '47, and '49. Then when they played in eight series throughout the 1950s I watched every one of them on television. But suddenly I wasn't rooting for the best and the strongest anymore. I wanted to see the teams who were playing the Yankees have a chance at winning. And when I'd see my own players, the ones who weren't that gifted but who were working hard, my heart would go out to them. At times I'd get discouraged because I'd want to give a chance to some of these guys who were average or below average. I wanted to play them, to let them have their day of glory, but there was always the pressure, the relentless pressure to win.

As a young football coach there were plenty of times when I didn't have the best judgment. Sometimes I was just plain too tough on my players. I'd work them harder than I needed to or I'd discipline them a little too harshly if they broke training rules. In the dining hall students were required to wear a shirt with a collar and socks. One night one of the players came into dinner without socks and I didn't let him eat there again for one whole month.

Now, from watching the girls work with Johnny, I was becoming more tolerant, more compassionate, and it was carrying over into my work. If a player needed a little extra help or time to learn something, I would give it to him. If a guy was having a problem at home, with his girlfriend or with his parents, I found myself listening a little longer, wanting to help.

By the late fall of 1965 we had just been shut out of our last three games and our annual Thanksgiving Day battle against Texas was looming ahead. Any idealism I had about my new job was fading. I was tense and tired, and as I pulled into the driveway one night the girls and Ruth Ann ran out and greeted me. They were giggling and tugging at me to go to the backyard, but all I wanted to do was go inside, take a shower, and sit down to dinner. Johnny was nowhere in sight. The girls looped their arms around me and walked me around to the back of the house. Johnny was standing on the patio, holding on to General. He looked over and smiled at me. And then suddenly he let go of the dog and walked like a drunken sailor clear across the patio. When Johnny got to the other end all by himself, he turned, looked back at me, and clapped his hands together. He started giggling, then laughing loudly. I dropped my briefcase and stood there stunned, and then I ran over to him and hugged him and I started laughing, too.

We both laughed and hugged until we couldn't laugh anymore. I just couldn't believe it! The whole family cheered as we hugged one another, clapped, and carried on. There was so much commotion our neighbors must have thought there was a football game going on in our backyard. Anna Lee was especially thrilled — she kept jumping up and down and telling Johnny to walk some more. That night at dinner she sat next to me and beamed as she said,

"Our hard work paid off, Daddy." I think that day was one of the happiest days in her life.

A few days later at the Thanksgiving Day game our team pulled together and we were playing beautifully. As the second quarter began we found ourselves starting a new possession deep in our own territory. After a 1-yard run on first down I decided the time was right for an unusual play that my assistant Jack Hurlburt and I had invented for the game. We called the risky trick play the "Texas Special." I felt that now was the time to use it and I had no doubt we could pull it off. Our quarterback, Harry Ledbetter, took the snap and threw a lateral pass to our flanker back, Jim Kauffman. He and our entire line kicked the dirt in disgust as if the pass were actually incomplete. At the same time, some 40 yards downfield, our split end, Dude McLean, broke from his fly pattern and then sprinted past the Texas defenders, who were shocked. Kauffman then hurled a long pass downfield to a wide-open McLean, who ran for a 91-yard touchdown. As I watched the thrilling sight of McLean sprinting down practically the entire length of the field, I thought about Johnny walking across our patio just a few days before.

Suddenly I clenched my fists, threw my arms up in the air, and let out a cheer so loud that it startled me as McLean crossed the goal line, threw the ball into the ground, and hugged his teammates. By halftime we were leading 17–0 and I thought for sure we had the game sewn up, but Texas came back from behind to win 21–17.

Later that week the coaches, players, and I sat and watched McLean on a game film running down the length of the field over and over again. That play turned out to be the longest scoring pass in Southwest Conference history, a record that held until 1985. For the first time I could really see the triumphant expressions on McLean's teammates' faces as they celebrated the touchdown. It was the same look I had seen on my girls' faces just days before as Johnny teetered across the fifteen feet of flagstone.

CHAPTER 4

TOUGH TIMES

BY late 1965, the war in Vietnam was heating up. Now, every night when I'd come home from work and turn on the television news, I'd watch as student demonstrators staged sit-ins on college campuses across the country, protesting the United States involvement, while far away from those campuses soldiers occupied small Vietnamese villages. The fighting between the North and South Vietnamese, which had started on a small scale, was growing into a full-scale war, and the United States was sending combat forces over to help the South Vietnamese.

Meanwhile, recruiting at A&M was becoming increasingly difficult because suddenly young people weren't interested in attending military schools anymore. They didn't want to go back to their hometowns after four years and have people say that now they'd have to go to war. The military was becoming more and more unpopular with many young people, and now when we played schools like Ohio State, in Columbus, where there was a great deal of student unrest, state troopers guarded our plane while we played the game. Though the mood of the country was tense, I thought that the recruiting would eventually get easier, and I was optimistic that things would soon turn around and we'd start winning more football games.

Ruth Ann and the children were making friends and we were all beginning to feel more and more comfortable in College Station. Our neighbors, Martha and Clyde Hargrove, had children the ages of our children and they all played together. Martha had a medical background and was a great support for Ruth Ann when she had questions or was worried about Johnny's heart. One evening we were invited to astronaut Alan Bean's house for dinner with some other coaches and their wives. Bean would eventually pilot the lunar module *Intrepid* on the Apollo 12 mission, the second moon landing in 1969. The minute we walked in the door we knew that we wanted to build a French country house just like his, with a steep roofline, dark shutters and arches, and brick floors. The next day he drove over to our house and generously handed us the architect's plans, and soon we started construction on a wooded acre in Bryan.

By the end of the year our dream home was completed. We found ourselves walking around each room and marveling at how spacious and beautiful it was. Ruth Ann took a lot of time picking out wallpaper patterns, choosing paint colors, and putting down carpeting. But we soon found out that there were few children in the neighborhood — just a lot of older people. By the following fall Jackie, two, and Johnny, four, had become even more important to each other, as Anna Lee and Laurie went off to school every day. Jackie was showing us all what an active imagination she had, and soon we discovered that she and Johnny had an imaginary pig to play with. The pig ate mush that they made out of twigs, dirt, and water. They'd run into the house to get mixing bowls, spoons, and water and then they'd sit at the breakfast table and stir up the mush and then go to the back of the yard and pretend they were feeding the pig. When I'd come home from work, they'd tell me to take my shoes off and walk softly in the backyard so I wouldn't disturb him.

Finally, after watching them play like this, Ruth Ann and I decided that the children needed a real pig to play with. One Sunday we drove out into the countryside and came home with Twiggy sitting in our backseat. The children immediately dressed him up in earmuffs and Laurie's pink tutu and carted him around the yard and all through the neighborhood in their round "moon wagon."

They were thrilled with Twiggy, but as he grew he started digging holes the size of small craters in the backyard and eating everything in sight. He didn't fit into Laurie's tutu anymore and quickly became much too big for the wagon. The children cried when we told them that we had to give him away, and it was with great sadness that we put him in the back of the car and took him back to where we first got him. Our yard was such a mess that I needed someone to help put it back together. I asked Lee Cooper, an older man who worked at Kyle Stadium tidying up and mowing the lawn, if he could help me with my yard work and mow the grass.

Lee came out to the house one afternoon to mow the lawn, and after he had been out there a while Johnny went and got his little wooden lawn mower and came right up next to him and they mowed the lawn together. Lee was always singing, and that afternoon while he pushed his mower, he taught Johnny the words to "Itsy Bitsy Spider" and "The Ballad of Davy Crockett." Pretty soon Johnny started asking for Lee almost every day. Like Elmer, Lee was gentle and kind to Johnny and he genuinely seemed to enjoy spending time with my son. Whenever I'd see Lee over at the stadium he'd always ask me, "How's that boy of yours doin', Coach?"

In the fall of 1966, it was time for Jackie to start preschool, which meant leaving Johnny behind. Johnny started looking forward to Lee's visits more than ever, especially now that Lee brought Cokes over when he came to the house. After he and Johnny had mowed the lawn together they'd sit outside, drink the Cokes, and visit. Lee would sit on our back steps, shoot marbles, and sing with Johnny for hours.

One afternoon after Lee left, Johnny and General were playing outside in the backyard. Ruth Ann kept peeking out the window to make sure they were okay, and then she'd go back to entertaining friends who were visiting. The third time she looked out the window she noticed that four or five children had joined Johnny. She had never seen them before. Since there were few children in the neighborhood, she was excited to see the children, who looked like they were between the ages of five and eight, running around the yard, playing tag.

When she checked up on them a few minutes later she saw that the children had formed a circle around Johnny and they were singing something. She opened the window so she could hear their song better. Instead she heard the sweet-looking children chanting, "You're so retarded, you're so retarded!" Johnny was unable to respond and he sat in the middle of the circle with a sad look on his little face while the children surrounded him and taunted him.

Ruth Ann was furious and stormed out to the yard. When the children saw her coming, they started to run away. She glanced over at Johnny, who was now sitting by himself, his arms crossed tight against his chest. "Children," Ruth Ann called out in a stern voice, clapping her hands, "come here right now and sit down."

Sheepishly the children came back and sat down on the grass. "I didn't like what I heard," she started.

One of the children blurted out, "He can't talk!"

Another little boy wearing a baseball cap said, "He's kind of scary."

"He's stupid," said a little girl with blond braids who couldn't have been more than five years old.

Ruth Ann held Johnny on her lap as she tried to explain to them that even though he looked a little different from them and acted a little different, he was more like them than not. Johnny put his arms around her and snuggled up close. This was the first of several times over the years when Ruth Ann would find herself telling children, "When you are mean and say unkind things, it hurts Johnny.

You may not realize it, but it does. How do you feel when someone calls you a bad name? He has emotions, he can be hurt, just the same as you. But he also has a lot of fun and he likes to play. And you know, he's very important to God, just as you're very important to God." The children sat on the ground cross-legged and listened attentively. When she finished talking, Johnny jumped off Ruth Ann's lap, went over to one of the little boys, took the child's hand, and said, "Play now."

The children jumped up to play with him, acting as if nothing had happened. One of them tagged Johnny and they were off playing their games. They all ran around the backyard a little more until they got tired and headed home.

That night Ruth Ann and I talked late into the night about Johnny's sweet and gentle nature. Johnny didn't even know how to be mean. We always worried that if a child came up and pinched or hit him, not only would he be hurt, but he would also learn bad habits. Here these children had been making fun of him, yet all he wanted was someone to play with and keep him company.

Eventually we found that the children who were invited over by our girls probably accepted Johnny a little more readily than the children who weren't as familiar with him. And if they made fun of him behind his back and said unkind things about his looks or the way he behaved, Anna Lee and Laurie would quickly defend their brother. But when their friends saw how the girls would play dolls and sit Johnny down so that he'd always be a part of their game, they wanted to play with him, too, and they started to like him a lot. Sometimes he'd come out of their bedroom wearing a funny old wig or some frilly clothes. They'd dress him up as a girl, a clown, a prince, or a princess. Johnny loved the attention we gave him as he paraded around in his different outfits. He was their plaything and they adored him. They pulled him in their wagon and made up imaginary friends together.

But it wasn't just the children who didn't know what to say or how to act. There were plenty of times when I felt uneasy when we were out in public with Johnny. He still made a lot of strange noises, grunts, and groans. Often when we'd be out strolling in the neighborhood with him or walking down the street in town, people would stop and stare, first looking at him and then at us.

Johnny was prone to wandering and I think this was because he'd do things on impulse, unaware of the consequences. We were so worried about his safety that we installed a chain lock on his bedroom door and locked him in during the day when he took naps, and when he was sleeping at night. At times we felt as though we were treating him like a caged animal. He was very persistent and there would be times when he'd get into the kitchen drawer and we'd take away a dangerous knife and a few minutes later we'd turn our backs and he'd have that same knife right back out again. When we would get angry with Johnny for carrying the kitten by the tail or getting into dangerous things or breaking something at a friend's house, the girls defended him and tried to make us feel awful as we attempted, not always successfully, to discipline him. We were constantly training and retraining him, trying to make him understand that he could get hurt.

Our bedroom was downstairs and the children's rooms were upstairs. Johnny would stand up on his bed and call down to us in a sad, loud voice, almost like a moan —"Mama, Pop"— during the middle of the day or at night. When we had company over, we always worried that people thought we were chaining him in. Ruth Ann and I felt constant pressure from other people. We didn't want them to think that we were mistreating him in any way, and there were times when it seemed that others were critical of the way we treated Johnny. We wasted a lot of time worrying about how other people felt instead of how Johnny was feeling.

Our close friends would go out of their way to tell us how precious and adorable Johnny was. We loved hearing that because we thought so, too. We deeply admired his fierce determination to

learn simple tasks that were difficult for him, to love others generously who might not love him back, or to walk or run when he was
really exhausted and would rather just lie down.

Mammy was very expressive about her love for Johnny, and she
was the first person we called whenever we wanted to discuss something about him, or when we just needed to brag about him. All
year we would look forward to our visits to her house in June. Johnny
was excited about seeing her, too, not only because he adored her,
but because he knew that she would give him a brand-new plastic
swimming pool on his birthday, just like she did every June 11.

In the beginning of June after spring practice, we'd load up the
station wagon. The four girls would sit in the back, and Johnny
would be settled in his flimsy little car seat in between Ruth Ann
and me. We'd make the five-hour trip, driving through "back country," an area right outside of town where there was on old railroad
bed, and then on through the small towns of Palestine, Canton,
Athens, and finally into Paris. We could count on Mammy being in
the same spot, always sitting out on the porch swing waiting for us.
She would be wearing a long apron that went down to her ankles
and she would be reading the newspaper. We'd leap out of the car
and the children would run up and hug her while I'd climb up on
top of the car and lower the suitcases down, one at a time, to Ruth
Ann. Then we'd settle in at Mammy's.

As we carried our suitcases into the house, wonderful smells
from the kitchen of meat cooking and pies baking greeted us. We
would hurriedly unpack, wash up, and go in to dinner. Without
fail, Mammy had a roast beef dinner with mashed potatoes, gravy,
biscuits, and an apple or lemon pie waiting for us. The table would
be set with her best dishes, but she never worried about the children
breaking them. Always in the middle of the table there would be a
bouquet of flowers from her garden. Then after dinner we'd plop
down on the overstuffed blue sofa in the living room. Ruth Ann

would fill Mammy in on all the children's latest news and the goings-on in College Station while I'd sit back and fall sound asleep, temporarily forgetting about the trouble I was having recruiting. Mammy would get out her books or a jigsaw puzzle and the children would sit with her for hours and play or read until bedtime. The routine was always the same, every night that we were there. There were no phone calls for us, or late-night meetings for me, and best of all we didn't have to prove ourselves every time we met someone new and worry about how they would react to Johnny. We were able to relax at Mammy's with Johnny in a way that seemed impossible in College Station. Mammy made such a fuss over him and the girls that we had nothing to do but enjoy them.

Every day Mammy sat in a lawn chair right next to her gorgeous purple hydrangea bushes, underneath the two large pecan trees in her yard, and watched Johnny play. He'd splash around in his little pool, roll over on his belly until it had touched the bottom, and then he'd pretend he was a big fish, and when his head would eventually go under, Mammy would dash over and lift him out of the pool. Half the time a neighborhood dog would wander in the yard and jump in with him, and they'd become best friends. I was constantly moving the pool from one part of the yard to another because it was killing Mammy's grass. But she didn't care. All she wanted was for Johnny to have fun.

When he had finished his swimming for the day she would get out her big old metal tub and fill it with just a little bit of water and then she'd watch Johnny dump buckets of dirt in the tub and make mud pies. He would sling mud every which way and she'd let him get as dirty as he wanted. He played like this for hours. Often he'd come into the house so covered with dirt and mud that he looked like a piglet. He'd even climb up on her lap and when she stood up her flowered summer dress would be covered with mud.

One afternoon Ruth Ann, the girls, and I decided to go down

the street and pay a visit to Hoot Gibson, my old basketball coach, and his wife, Jean. Johnny was having such a good time with Mammy that we asked her if she wouldn't mind watching him while we were gone. We hadn't been gone more than fifteen minutes when she couldn't find Johnny. She had run into the house to answer the phone and when she returned he was gone. She searched the yard and the house calling out his name but there was no answer. While she stood in the hallway, calling for him, she heard muffled sounds coming from the small bathroom downstairs. She jiggled the bathroom door but it wouldn't open. Johnny sounded scared and he was crying, "Mammy, Mammy, get me out!" She banged on the door and jiggled it some more but she couldn't get it open. Finally, she phoned us at Hoot and Jean's but she couldn't get an answer because Hoot had just gotten a new car and we were out taking a ride in it.

She had no choice but to call the fire department because the bathroom didn't have an outside window for her to crawl into. In a few minutes she heard the wail of sirens and two brand-new shiny fire trucks pulled up to the house. Six firemen wearing long black coats and carrying axes came tearing through the door. They ran right past Mammy and started up the stairs. But she stopped them and showed them where Johnny was. By this time he was crying really hard, and the firemen wasted no time in breaking the door down with their axes.

When we returned home, an hour later, Mammy and Johnny were quietly sitting at the kitchen table eating graham crackers and drinking chocolate milk. Mammy had an amused look on her face when she told us what had happened. It was no big deal to her. I went down to the hardware store the next day, bought a new door, and installed it for her.

At the end of the day Johnny and Mammy would go into her back bedroom downstairs and read together. Johnny's favorites were the Dr. Seuss books, and Mammy read *Green Eggs and Ham* so many times that he memorized most of the book. "I am Sam. Sam I am. That Sam-I-am! That Sam-I-am!" we'd hear him saying to himself years later. Though at times none of us could really understand Johnny, we'd always hear him giggling and making happy sounds in Mammy's bedroom. They had a special way of communicating with each other.

He had such a hard time expressing himself verbally, and the first summer we were at Mammy's house we noticed that when Johnny wanted something and we couldn't understand him he would act it out. If he wanted a sandwich and Mammy didn't understand him, he'd pretend to take a piece of bread in one hand and a knife in the other and he'd make a motion like he was slathering peanut butter on bread. Or, if he wanted to swim, he'd move his arms like he was doing the breast stroke. And he was becoming a wonderful mimic. A friend of ours smoked, and when he wanted to talk about her, he'd act like he was smoking a cigarette. Or if was trying to talk about Laurie, he'd shrug his shoulders and furrow his eyebrows in just the same way that she did. He learned how to impersonate almost anyone.

He also found a new way to entertain us all by taking two wire coat hangers, placing the hooked ends on the tips of his thick index and middle fingers, and getting them swinging so they would go back and forth. He'd get them going fast, then slower, and he'd keep them going sometimes for an hour. His little "act" was mesmerizing and the children in Mammy's neighborhood would come over to watch him as he got the hangers swinging into a circular rhythm. All of us tried to do it. We tried for hours but we couldn't get the hang of it. So far I've never seen anyone master the "hanger trick" except for Johnny. From time to time I'd shut my office door on a slow day and try to do his trick, but I'd have absolutely no luck. To this day, I just can't figure out how he could perform such a stunt.

CHAPTER 5

BIG WINS / LITTLE VICTORIES

JOHNNY was getting cuter by the minute. His hair had turned a platinum blond and his clear blue eyes seemed to light up any room he walked into. He was a happy guy and he smiled and giggled constantly. But he moved slowly and was much smaller than children his age. Although he was five, people always thought he was at least two years younger than he was.

With all of his siblings off at school, Johnny was the only child home. He walked around the house during the day calling Jackie's name and playing with her toys, and we had no idea how to find other children for him to play with. It became obvious that we desperately needed a place to send him. Finally, we called the local board of education, asking them if they knew anything about schooling for a five-year-old boy with Down syndrome. They told us they'd get back to us with information, but we never heard from them again. We asked some people in the education department at A&M if they could help us, but no one had any answers for us, and one administrator asked us why we'd even consider sending our son to school. They couldn't tell us about any schools or programs for special needs children. We even looked up schools in the Yellow Pages with no luck. Even though we were living in a college town and there were plenty of educational programs, we found nothing for Johnny.

One day while Ruth Ann told our neighbor about our struggles to find the right school for Johnny, she suggested that we might find a program through the Bryan Association for Retarded Citizens. Simply walking into the office with the big red sign on the door that read "BRYAN ASSOCIATION FOR RETARDED CITIZENS" was humiliating. In a way, it was the first time that we had to officially acknowledge that Johnny wasn't "normal." Still, we were excited when they told us about a small program for children with disabilities in nearby Bryan.

But from the beginning we didn't have a good feeling about the place. As we walked Johnny down the halls of his new school we were aware that the small brick building that housed the ten or so students needed a lot of repair. The teacher who greeted us smiled politely when we brought Johnny into the classroom, yet she made no effort to introduce him to the other children, most of whom had mental disabilities.

Johnny didn't seem to mind going to school. But, we were troubled that the classroom had only two windows and was on the dark side of the building, and the walls were painted a dull, depressing beige color. The children's artwork wasn't displayed anywhere. After a few months we realized that the children weren't learning anything. The program was mostly baby-sitting. Often when we'd go to pick Johnny up he'd be sitting in the middle of the floor holding a ball, not really talking to anyone. We felt vaguely ashamed that he was going to such a school, and as we came and went we kept a low profile, often avoided talking to the other parents. But at least on Tuesdays and Thursdays, the only days the school operated,

Johnny was seeing children other than his sisters. And Ruth Ann was getting a little time to herself — something she desperately needed.

Just getting Johnny out of the house and to school in the mornings was a major victory for Ruth Ann. She'd have the three girls dressed, fed, and waiting in the backseat of the car for her, and as she finished up some last-minute detail in the house, Johnny would stand right in front of her and start to take his clothes off, or disappear into the bathroom to play in the sink or brush his teeth again. She'd have to dress him for the second or third time that morning, put him in the car, and race off to the girls' school so they wouldn't be late and then on over to Johnny's school. One day after she had dropped off the girls and arrived at Johnny's school, she got out of the car first and as she went around to the other side of the car to let Johnny out she saw him locking the car doors. She knocked on the door, and smiled at him, hoping he'd open it so that she could get him into school. But he just shook his head and smiled back at her — he was playing a funny joke on Mom and enjoying himself immensely. After fifteen minutes of pleading and sweet-talking, Ruth Ann finally got him to unlock the door, and she carried him to his classroom.

Some of the children in the school knew how to perform tasks like tying their shoes and riding a bike. Johnny wanted to learn how to do these things, too, and he had sisters who were more than willing to teach him. After they finished their homework at night, Laurie and Anna Lee rigged shoelaces on their bedposts and they'd sit up on the bed and make him practice tying. They'd stay up half the night while he tried over and over again to learn to make loops and tie a knot. He was as determined to learn as they were to teach him, but the ends of his fingers were so clubbed that he had no dexterity and he didn't learn to tie until he was nearly six. What he lacked in dexterity, though, he made up for with his wonderful flexibility. Sometimes I'd go into his room and he would be lying

80

in bed with his legs pulled up over his stomach in such a way that would enable him to breathe more easily. It also helped if he sat up, his legs extended straight out in front of him, with his head resting on his knees. It was scary to watch him, always struggling to get his breath.

On weekends the girls would take him out and spend half the day teaching him to ride a bike. They used Laurie's old nineteen-inch bike with training wheels and would run back and forth on the blacktop in front of our house, holding on to the bike as Johnny tried to get the hang of pedaling. One Saturday in the late fall after a football game, I went outside and Johnny was running around the street, playing with the girls. Although it was a chilly day, they had all gotten overheated running, and the girls had taken their sweaters, shoes, and socks off and so had Johnny. Our doctors always warned us to be careful with him, to treat him with "kid gloves." "Johnny will probably be sick all the time," most of them said. They told us to dress him warmly and make sure he didn't overexert himself. I started to tell Johnny to stop running and put his shoes and socks on, but I stopped myself. Instead, I sat down on the curb and watched the children play. They were having so much fun, laughing and carrying on, that I didn't say a word.

I realized that those were always my happiest times, when I allowed Johnny to live right there in the moment. He was free to run and play. At these times, Ruth Ann and I would forget to take his pulse.

The girls would push him hard to learn things and eventually he would. When he finally learned to ride a bike, it was with training wheels. Maybe he could have gone a step further and learned to ride without the training wheels, but then we'd stop pushing. We would remember the doctors' cautions about dressing him warmly and taking his pulse constantly, and once again we'd worry that maybe we were bad parents.

Football season was always an extremely strenuous time of the year for our family, and I was tense about leaving Ruth Ann at home alone for long hours with four young children. She desperately needed some time to herself. On Sundays she liked to go to church and have an hour of quiet time, her only time alone all week. I sometimes couldn't go with her because of meetings or special events I had to attend. A member of our congregation, Bob Mullinex, noticed one Sunday that Ruth Ann was by herself with all of the children. After the service Bob, who lived a few miles away, offered to take Johnny to his house the following Sunday. He had some horses in his backyard and he thought Johnny might enjoy seeing them. Bob showed Johnny how he groomed his horses, and some Sundays he'd hoist Johnny up on one of his horses and lead him around his backyard.

Bob was a quiet, unassuming guy who owned an air-conditioning business. Here I was spending my days looking for the best — the toughest, fastest players — players who would contribute to my team's winning. Now all of a sudden I was looking at an ordinary guy who just happened to have a huge heart, and his kindness was helping us out. He would take his own time — something none of us have a lot of — to enjoy my son. Bob and Johnny discovered that they both loved the color red, and often Johnny would come back from Bob's house with a red handkerchief, shirt, or hat. Then, every Christmas a big gift wrapped in shiny red paper would arrive at our door. Inside would be a pair of brand-new red pajamas, the kind with the flap on the back and with built-in feet. The card always read: "Merry Christmas. Love, from Santa Bob." Fifteen years later Johnny still talked about Bob Mullinex. Because of guys like Bob, Elmer, and Lee, I found myself slowly having a greater appreciation for people who showed Johnny and our family small acts of kindness. I realized that they made such a big difference in our lives.

If there was one other constant support during those years it was our new pediatric cardiologist, Dan McNamara, who had come highly recommended by our pediatrician. He was based ninety miles away, at Texas Children's Hospital, in Houston. We were still concerned that Johnny could die any minute and we wanted to see if there was anything more that we could do for him, other than taking his pulse and giving him digitalis. Most of Dr. McNamara's patients were children who had serious heart problems, and I don't think there was anyone who understood Johnny's heart condition as well as this pediatrician did.

Because Johnny had to be monitored very closely, we saw Dr. McNamara the first few weeks we were in College Station and then continued to have yearly checkups. Johnny continued to have shortness of breath and was often turning blue, especially in his extremities. We desperately wanted Dr. McNamara to give us some definitive answers, but instead he offered us the warm support that very few doctors know how to give. No doubt we had had some good doctors, but many of them had sort of patted Johnny and said things like, "Oh, isn't he cute?" But from Dr. McNamara we got true warmth.

I sensed that Johnny was an individual to Dr. McNamara, a real valuable little person. Not too many people reacted to our son that way. I thought of the time when I got home early from practice one warm spring afternoon and Ruth Ann, the children, and I went to a playground near our house. The minute we arrived the children threw their sweaters down on the ground and started to climb on the equipment. Anna Lee and Laurie helped Johnny get up on the swing, ride on the seesaw, and climb up the slide. I noticed how the other parents around us kept looking at Johnny, who was so frail, small, and different looking than their children. As I'd realized countless other times, I knew that these parents hadn't seen many children with Down's and I could tell that they felt sorry for us. For some reason that day I was especially aware of how these parents would turn away when, studying Johnny, they would catch Ruth Ann or me looking at them. I was sure that in their minds Johnny was a pathetic, strange-looking little boy. People often reacted this way, but every time they did, it surprised and hurt me just like it was happening for the very first time. Johnny was merely our son, the girls' brother, and a child who was sometimes wonderful, sometimes exasperating, but a vital part of the Stallings family.

Dr. McNamara cared for Johnny as an individual and not just another child with Down syndrome. As soon as we walked in, he would hoist Johnny up on his knee, cuddle with him, and make us feel that he was the most precious and lovable child in the world. He called Johnny by name, and when he examined him, he did so with great care and respect. His calm and loving manner made us feel like everything was going to work out. He'd say, "Just live with him, love him, and enjoy him." Now, maybe for the first time, we had some hope that he would live longer, but this wasn't based on anything scientific.

He never gave us any idea how long Johnny would live. Sometimes we wondered whether we should attempt heart surgery. We would get ourselves in turmoil over it. Ruth Ann, especially, read medical books constantly. For some reason that I'm not quite sure of, I was a little more accepting of the doctors' opinions than she was. After all, I reasoned, they had spent years studying and working with children who had these problems, and I had to trust that they knew what they were doing. We would go back and forth about what was best for Johnny until we were in turmoil. Finally Dr. McNamara made us realize that we shouldn't attempt surgery. We had to get on with our lives and stop putting things on hold. He liberated us with his words, and we finally began to relax a little.

For the first time since Johnny was born, Ruth Ann hired a baby-sitter and would go out a few afternoons a week to take painting lessons or have lunch with friends. We began to go out to dinner once in a while, just the two of us, or to a movie. And Ruth Ann started playing the piano again after not touching it for years. She had taught piano while she was in college, and during those years she had gone back to our high school and worked in the music department and taught band instruments. She would always get us tickets to the civic music series when we were in high school. Music had been such an important part of her life, and now when I'd come home some nights I'd find the children gathered around the piano and Ruth Ann would be playing all sorts of show tunes. The girls and Johnny would hum along while she sang, until pretty soon they had learned the words to more than a dozen songs. Then she taught them the words and music to many of the hymns we sang in church.

More and more we were getting used to Johnny's blue periods, the times when the tips of his fingers and his face looked exceptionally blue. These times also seemed to be less frequent, maybe due to the digitalis that he was still taking, and we stopped monitoring his pulse so closely. The digitalis seemed to control his shortness of breath to some extent, too. I was beginning to worry a little less, to listen in awe as he remembered the words to a song and sang it loud and clear.

So much of the last five years had been taken up with repeating instructions over and over again. I knew a certain amount of that went along with parenting, but it had been particularly true with raising Johnny. How many times had I heard Ruth Ann say: "Johnny, flush the toilet. Johnny, say thank you. Johnny, don't hurt the cat. Johnny, put that knife down, it will hurt you." She must have been ready to burst at times, but she always used a calm, patient tone of voice when she told the children for the sixth time to clean up their room or to get off the telephone or when she tried to teach them manners. I really can't begin to imagine her daily frustrations with the job of being a full-time mother raising four children, yet over the years she never seemed any more agitated with Johnny.

From an early age she had insisted that all the children have household chores. Anna Lee set the table every night, Laurie folded the laundry, Jackie took out the trash, and Johnny's job was to vacuum. She made sure that he did his job twice a week and that it was done thoroughly even if that meant going over and over the same spots.

We were beginning to laugh together a little more easily as a family, and I started thinking that Johnny might very well live for a while longer. But even as I was loosening up and learning to enjoy him more, things were anything but relaxed during the day at work.

We opened the '67 season against SMU in College Station. It was a nationally televised game. We were ahead late in the game, but SMU edged us out, 20–17.

The next three games were also close, but we still lost each of them. Then our luck began to change during our fifth game, against Texas Tech. We were playing in Lubbock and had just given up a late Tech touchdown in the fourth quarter. Things were about as tense as they could be. We trailed 24–21 with less than a minute left in the game. Then, with just 11 seconds remaining and facing a fourth and 15 situation at the Tech 45 yard line, our quarterback Edd Hargett passed deep down into the middle of the field. Bob Long, our wideout, leaped up out of the crowd of defenders and made an unbelievable catch on the Tech 15 yard line. On the game's final play Hargett rolled to his left to throw but all receivers were covered. Despite wearing braces on both knees, he raced for the right corner of the end zone. Larry Stegent made a great block and we scored as the clock ran out. This spectacular victory marked a turning point for our team, and we went on to win seven consecutive games that fall, taking the Southwest Conference championship before going on to the Cotton Bowl on New Year's Day in 1968. The last time that A&M had played in the Cotton Bowl was in 1942, so the fans were really thrilled.

It was a really big game, even bigger for me because we were playing against Alabama. I was the pupil pitted against the teacher, the best teacher of them all, Coach Bryant. We had been in close touch during the previous few years, mostly by telephone. Of course, we always talked about football, but he liked to talk about other things, too. He loved playing the stock market, and he would call and tell me about a stock I should buy until pretty soon he had me hooked. We were now headed into the height of the bull market, and I started calling him once or twice a month with a tip or two. Whenever we had a conversation he always asked me how Johnny was doing. After we lost a game, I knew Coach Bryant would be calling. He would say, "Bebes, you don't need any friends when you're winning."

Alabama once again was highly ranked nationally and their 8–2 season that year was certainly better than A&M's. Most so-called experts (the media, oddsmakers, and commentators) said there was no question that Alabama would win. Sportswriters had a field day with the 1968 Cotton Bowl game both before and afterward.

Usually at bowls each coach holds a press conference individually, but the press covering this game, as well as the executives and the director of the Cotton Bowl, thought it would be more interesting if Coach Bryant and I had joint press conferences at the Sheraton in downtown Dallas where our team stayed. Alabama practiced in the morning and A&M practiced in the afternoon, so I'd come to the press conferences straight from the practice field. One afternoon when I arrived, there was Coach Bryant surrounded by members of the media. He was dressed fit to kill in a Hickey-Freeman suit and alligator shoes. I walked in wearing khakis, sneakers, and a windbreaker. Coach Bryant noticed me and told the media, "I refuse to have my picture taken with anybody that looks that bad." Everybody got a good laugh out of that.

During that press conference all the reporters addressed their questions to Coach Bryant. He'd interrupt them and say, "Why doesn't anyone ask Bebes a question?" The writers laughed some more and the next day they asked for another joint conference. That's when I decided I'd outdress him. I took a tuxedo to practice with me that afternoon, and after practice I put it on and headed over to the press conference. When I walked in all the writers were buzzing around Coach Bryant because there he sat with a cowboy hat on, his shirt opened at the collar and a bright scarf tied around his neck, and on his feet, propped up on an ottoman, were cowboy boots with "Texas Aggies," written on the side. They were obviously a gift he'd received from some Aggie alumnus while he was coaching there. All of the photographers were busy snapping pictures of his boots, and not one person even noticed that I was wearing a tux! Once again, I lost.

At 6:30 A.M. on New Year's Day — game day — I opened the curtains to our room at the Hilton Inn on Mockingbird Lane and Central Expressway in Dallas and looked down on the parking lot below. Freezing rain and sleet beat steadily against the windowpanes. But even though it was dark and miserable outside, I was just as excited as could be as I put on my jacket and tie, laced up my work boots, and went down to the hotel lobby. I stood in the lobby sipping coffee from a Styrofoam cup, watching out the window as the wind swept the puddles from one side to the other on the blacktop. I was waiting for the players to come down for their nine o'clock pregame breakfast. I felt an unusual tension because there was so much at stake in this particular game. Plenty had been written about teacher versus pupil, and I certainly didn't want to look bad — especially with all the media hype.

I didn't have much appetite for our steak and egg breakfast that morning, and as I moved around the team, I noticed that they weren't eating well either. We left the hotel around ten-thirty because with so much traffic in town I was worried that the usual ten-to fifteen-minute trip to the Cotton Bowl, near downtown Dallas at Fair Park, the site of the big Texas state fair, might take us at least half an hour, even though we had police escorts. The game was scheduled for one o'clock, but as a rule of thumb I've always liked to get to the stadium two hours before game time. Before long we went out to a packed house — seventy-five thousand fans — and millions more watching the game on national television.

Alabama opened the scoring with an 80-yard, 10-play drive, taking the lead 7–0. Three minutes later we tied the score. By halftime we were leading 13–10. The knot in my stomach eased, and I knew we could play with them. We had moved the ball well in the first half, and I was pleased with both our passing and running games. Our quarterback Edd Hargett, who would be named the game's outstanding back, threw twenty passes and completed half of them, two for touchdowns. I was cautiously optimistic. I looked across the field at Coach Bryant, standing on the sidelines; his familiar houndstooth hat with the little red feather on the side was pulled down on his forehead so I could barely see his eyes and I wondered what he was thinking.

In the second half, we changed our game plan and stuck to the cold, hard ground, passing only once. The pressure was on the defense, and led by Billy Hobbs, Rolf Krugger, Jim Piper, Ivan Jones, Tommy Maxwell, and Curley Hallman, we time and again turned back the Crimson Tide on key plays. Soon we had extended our lead to 20–10. Running back Wendell Hously, who had been injured most of the regular season, was now back to the form that won him All-SWC honors the year before, and Alabama had a hard time stopping him. He broke at least five tackles on a fourth-quarter 20-yard run that enabled us to make our last and winning touchdown. Still, the outcome hung in the balance until the final 22 seconds, when Curley Hallman intercepted a desperate Snake Stabler pass.

We won 20–16, and before it even registered I could see Coach Bryant among the crowds spilling onto the field. His gait was a bit labored, probably from the arthritis in his hip, but I watched him working his way to the 50 yard line, where I was surrounded by my players. My heart was pounding. I looked at him and extended my hand when suddenly Coach Bryant threw his arms around my waist and lifted me at least two feet off the ground. My breath was knocked right out of me and I looked down at the players and then we all started laughing and yelling until Coach Bryant lowered me down. It was a heartfelt gesture because Coach Bryant hated losing with a passion; it was simply unacceptable to him. Yet I knew that he was proud that we had won. Ultimately he wanted the best for all of his "boys." Later he joked that he wasn't so much trying to congratulate me as to throw me to the ground.

After the game I held a press conference in the locker room. There must have been one hundred reporters crowded into that room. An A&M manager came by and called out, "Coach Bryant is coming, Coach Bryant is coming." I turned to the media and said, "You all will have to excuse me," and I headed toward Coach Bryant.

"You looking for me?" I asked him.

"No, I've seen all of you I want to see. I want to talk to the players." I watched, thrilled as he went around and visited with each member of our team. There was a hush in that room and the players treated Coach Bryant with reverence. He knew the right thing to say to every one of them; he was a true genius that way.

When I arrived back at the hotel Ruth Ann and the children stood in the doorway of our room to greet me. They all kissed me and Johnny wrapped his little arms around my legs. I started to pick him up but my fingers and toes were completely numb from the cold and I couldn't get a firm grip on him. The temperatures had fallen well below freezing that day and the first thing I did was take a hot shower. Later Johnny snuggled up on my lap while we all stayed up half the night to get the newspapers that came out at 3 A.M. I couldn't wait to see the headlines and I was dumb-founded when one of the Dallas newspapers' headline simply said, "BRYANT — GREAT IN DEFEAT." The news article barely mentioned A&M winning the game.

After winning the Southwest Conference and Cotton Bowl, I felt like I'd be at A&M forever. Everything was finally coming together with a team that had been losing, and after some miserable years of recruiting I was seeing results.

Johnny, too, was making great progress. He had finally gotten toilet trained. After years of accidents, often in public places like department stores and restaurants, Johnny at five and a half years old was finally out of diapers. He was proud of himself and he told everybody we knew, "No more diapers!"

A year later, in the early summer of 1969, before the end of spring training, the president of the First Bank & Trust in Bryan, Henry Clay, and I were having lunch at a local restaurant. We were talking about the usual things, football, interest rates, people we knew in common, when somewhere along the line Henry started talking about the best price of land in Texas. "The best county in Texas to buy land is in Lamar County," Henry said.

"No kidding? I grew up in Lamar County," I said.

"Well, I buy and sell farms and ranches in Lamar County all the time. You can get more for your dollar in Lamar County right now than any place in Texas. In fact, I've got two pieces of land that I'm trying to sell. One of them is nearly six hundred acres — you would probably really like that one. It's a vast expanse of rolling meadows. The other parcel is nearly twice the size and that is gorgeous, too." As we got up to leave, Henry said, "Next time you go back to Paris, maybe you'd like to look at one of them. Just give me a call before you go."

Ruth Ann and I had always wanted to own some land where we could raise cattle and have a few horses. Like many boys growing up in Texas, there were times when I saw myself as a sort of Gene Autry character, riding my horse bareback through hills and valleys, stopping only to eat, sleep, or play my harmonica — living the life of a cowboy. Now in the role of a highly pressured football coach I knew how important it was to have an escape and gain a little perspective as well as privacy. Maybe this was a good time to buy a piece of land.

Right after spring training we headed for Paris. I always loved taking most of the month of June off, and this time as the family piled into the station wagon, I felt an extra twinge of excitement. I couldn't stop thinking about Henry Clay's farms.

After we'd been at Mammy's house a few days and visited with our family and friends I was anxious to look at the land. I called my dad and asked him if he'd like to head over to the area north of Paris, toward the Red River, which divides Oklahoma and Texas, and see what this six-hundred-acre parcel of land looked like. Ten minutes later, he drove over and we all climbed in his car and headed out of town. It was a sparkling June day, and as we barreled along the country roads I felt like we were embarking upon a wonderful adventure. About ten minutes later we came to a small sign stuck haphazardly in the ground that said CLAY, and we jumped out of the car and inspected the rolling meadows. The land was vast, all right, but it looked kind of scraggly — there were no fences in some places, and where there were fences they were in desperate need of repair. Instead of the well-kept barns and outbuildings that I had envisioned, a tired little one-room cabin with a dilapidated screened front porch sat on a pretty little lake, all I'd ever need for fishing.

"You ought to bulldoze that thing down, Bebes," Dad said, pointing to the cabin. Right then, I felt defeated; maybe Dad was right — the cabin needed work, the land was overgrown, it wasn't perfect. I kicked a stone and thought, He knows what he's talking about. The land isn't really that great. But then Dad, Ruth Ann, and I walked to the other side of the cabin, where there was a big open meadow, and we watched as the children took their shoes and socks off and rolled down a small hill in the long grass. They were laughing and shouting and trying to catch grasshoppers. They would catch one, and then just as they thought it was securely in their hands it would fly right out. Suddenly, Johnny gasped as he saw a big toad hopping in the grass. Anna Lee and Laurie shot over to where it was and caught it for him. They showed him how to cup his little hands and then Anna Lee dropped the toad right into his palms. He was jumping up and down and yelling out, "I've got a froggie!" It was right then that I knew we just had to have this refuge. On the way home to Mammy's the children were in high spirits in the back of the car, and we had to stop several times just to calm them down. But I noticed that Ruth Ann was unusually quiet on the ride back. I kept glancing over at her while Dad and I talked about all of the things that needed to be done to the land. As we bumped along the country roads, she sat next to the open car window, her eyes closed as the wind blew through her hair.

That night after we had put the children to bed, we sat together out on Mammy's porch swing. I started to talk about the land, how we were going to afford it, what kinds of improvements we'd make, when Ruth Ann took my arm.

"Bebes, we're going to have another baby."

I put my feet down to stop the swing. "Ruth Ann, don't joke like that with me," I said and gave her a playful nudge and a kiss on the cheek.

"No, I'm not joking." She suddenly looked tired and fragile. "I went to Mammy's doctor, yesterday. It's true, Bebes. The baby is due in February." It had been five years since we had had a child. From time to time we had talked about wanting to have another baby and I'd hear Ruth Ann say, "A football coach needs a son who will play football." Maybe that's what I felt deep down inside, too. I guess our dream of having such a child took hold and never went away. But now, I wasn't sure how I felt.

"Well, this is really a surprise!" I kissed Ruth Ann. We sat quietly for a while holding hands.

"It's late now. Maybe we should go to bed," she said.

"If you don't mind, I think I'm just going to sit here for a little while longer. I'll be up in a few minutes." I sat in Mammy's porch swing, swaying back and forth, trying to sort out my feelings about another baby. I thought about our children — Anna Lee, Laurie, Johnny, and Jackie — and how they had been running around in the tall grass of the open meadows on the land we had seen earlier in the day. I remembered the toad the girls had caught for Johnny and how they had helped him put on his shoes and socks after they had been rolling in the grass. Anna Lee had carried him piggyback all the way back to the car. I tried to imagine a fifth child — maybe a little dark-haired boy running around and laughing with the children. But I just couldn't picture him. I fell asleep on the porch swing that night and woke up when Ruth Ann rubbed my shoulders and told me to come up to bed.

Once we got back to College Station I called Henry Clay and told him how much I liked his land. Soon we struck a deal. Almost immediately we bought some cattle and a couple of horses. We started driving the 250 miles to the land, which we called the farm, on the weekends. One weekend, Ruth Ann and I decided to give it a name. We asked the children for ideas as we drove along and we came up with the "Hike A-Way Ranch." We liked the double meaning of "hike" as a football term and in reference to our hiking on the farm.

Then we hired Henry Mullins, an old country farmer who lived nearby and who had worked for Henry Clay, to manage the property. Mr. Henry, as we called him, had the curious habit, as did others in East Texas, of wearing the same cotton pants and flannel shirt on July 4 as he did on January 4. He explained that they kept him cool in the summer and warm in the winter. He walked with a slight limp. I was told that he broke his ankle while stomping hay into a stationary hay press. Animals seemed to love him, and as soon as he'd start working out on the land he'd have all the cows trailing him. The children liked him, too, and they followed him around as he did his chores. He'd point out different kinds of birds or animals to them, taking a special amount of time showing Johnny these creatures.

And even though A&M had fallen to 3–7 during the previous season, I was still in good spirits. I thought we'd played a pretty tough schedule and that it was not representative of the team we had. Despite our record that year, nine members of our team were selected in the pro football draft, the second most from any college (Notre Dame had sent twelve). I was optimistic about the future.

But, we suffered another 3–7 season in 1969. More than ever I felt the need to get away from College Station, and we spent our first Christmas at the farm. It was a wonderful escape and I built king-sized bunk beds and put them in the only place they'd fit, right near the fireplace in our tiny cabin. The children slept on the bottom and Ruth Ann and I slept on the top bunks. She was very pregnant now and I'd have to help her climb up on the top bunk. During the middle of the night, I'd pull on my boots to go outside and bring in wood to stoke the fire. It would blaze up right near the beds and I'd spend half the night worrying that they were going to catch on fire. But when the fire died down we'd nearly freeze to death. It was our only source of heat, and we all huddled together to keep warm.

Right after the New Year we had to get back to College Station so that I could start scheduling my recruiting trips. The children had a great time at the farm. They played outside in the light dusting of snow we got and snuck their flashlights under the covers every night, telling ghost stories and giggling until they all fell asleep together. They hated leaving the farm, and I wasn't particularly anxious to get back to recruiting either. It seemed like it was getting more and more difficult. Military schools were still extremely unpopular, with no end to the Vietnam War in sight.

On February 18, 1970, Martha Kate Stallings was born at St. Joseph Hospital in Bryan. I had been on the road, and when Ruth Ann called me to say she was in labor I hopped right in the car and made it home just in time to get her to the hospital. Once again, she and I shared a momentary disappointment that we didn't have the little football player we had dreamed of. But throughout her pregnancy I had been troubled by conflicting feelings, wondering if it would be hard for another boy to live in our family. Johnny was so adored by his sisters and Ruth Ann and me. I thought that we might have a little boy whom we would try to turn into a football player, but he might not want to play, and that would have been frustrating for all of us. So, once again, I found myself thankful and happy to have a healthy baby girl. When we brought her home from the hospital Johnny couldn't wait to hold her. She was a big baby and we'd wrap her in a blanket, and as Johnny sat on the sofa and held her I could barely see his frail little body.

It was a happy time in our family and we were enjoying a new baby in the house after almost six years. But our relaxed attitude ended abruptly one Sunday night that fall while we were in church. Our family was sitting in the balcony and I was holding Johnny on my lap while Ruth Ann held the baby. As I bent my head during a prayer I saw a dark red stain spreading all over the sides of my gray flannel slacks. Instantly I lifted Johnny a couple of feet in the air and gasped so loudly that I startled myself and everyone around me. The blood looked like it was coming from his bottom and it was gushing. As I stood up I felt the wetness through my pants, and my legs suddenly felt heavy. Blood seemed to be everywhere; on the floor, on my hands, and all over my shoes. Johnny's little blue and white checked outfit was completely covered in a deep red stain.

I half whispered, half shouted to Ruth Ann. She looked up at me quizzically, and then when she saw all the blood, she cried out and grabbed the girls by the hand. We whisked them down the stairs to the main part of the church and without explanation, we plunked them in the back pew with the first friends we saw and ran out the front door. A trail of blood followed us, and I raced to the car clutching Johnny, with Ruth Ann running along at my side.

As I ran I looked down at my son. His little body started to feel limp in my arms and his eyes began to open and close. His normally pale face was white as a sheet. When we got to the car I gently put him down on the front seat and put my ear to his chest. I breathed easier as I heard the thump thump of his heart. "Johnny, say something to Pop, please. Johnny, say something to Pop," I pleaded.

"Sleep," Johnny answered weakly.

"No, don't go to sleep," said Ruth Ann as she smoothed his forehead with her hand. She reached down on the floor and picked up one of his favorite stuffed animals, Harry the dog. "It's okay, Johnny." She held Harry in front of Johnny and pretended the dog was talking to him. I had a phone in my car, which I mostly used when I was on the road recruiting. I picked it up, dialed the operator, and asked them to put me through to Bryan Hospital. With the accelerator floored, I sped to the hospital. Ruth Ann sang to Johnny, "Itsy bitsy spider went up the waterspout. Down came the rain and washed the spider out . . ." as she made the lively hand movements that go along with the song. We glanced at each other without speaking. It was clear what we were thinking. This is it, Johnny can't survive surgery, they can't open him up, he can't tolerate anesthesia, it will kill him, I said to myself repeatedly.

I was driving like a madman, running red lights and screeching around corners. By the time we reached the hospital emergency entrance, my hands had gripped the steering wheel so tight that they hurt when I lifted Johnny out of the car. Two orderlies in bright white jackets brusquely greeted us. They whisked Johnny away from me, placed him on a stretcher, and wheeled him into the hospital. Ruth Ann and I left the car right there in the emergency entrance with the keys in the ignition and followed closely behind as the orderlies ran ahead and shouted for the doctor.

A bunch of doctors and nurses were waiting for Johnny and they immediately wheeled an IV rack toward him. "Which one of you is in charge here?" I asked the group of medical personnel who encircled Johnny.

A tall, balding middle-aged man looked up at me. "I am the attending doctor." "My son can't have any kind of surgery," I said. "We've been told that the anesthesia could kill him."

The doctor peered at Ruth Ann and me over his glasses and then looked down at Johnny. He pressed on Johnny's stomach and then took his stethoscope out and listened to his chest. As he put his stethoscope away in the pocket of his white coat he said, "We're going to X-ray him. Please wait here." The orderlies wheeled him down the corridor. I looked at Johnny's little body on the big stretcher and I started to cry a little to myself. A few minutes later the doctor came out of the room with Johnny and said, "We've found the problem." I noticed beads of perspiration over his lips. "He's eaten a piece of glass."

"He doesn't put glass in his mouth," I said. I walked closer to the doctor and repeated, "He just doesn't do that."

The doctor led Ruth Ann and me into the X-ray room and insisted that I look at the X rays that were clipped up to a white box on the wall. I had no idea what I was looking at. All I saw was darkness against light in strange shapes. "There's something in there that looks like glass and we've got to get in there and take it out or your son isn't going to make it," the doctor said, pointing to a part of the X ray that was black.

I stood staring at the dark mass, squeezing Ruth Ann's hand. Was I going to insist that Johnny not be operated on? I looked up at the doctor and studied his horn-rimmed glasses, watching the lines in his forehead deepen as his expression became more serious. I hesitated. I had to believe that he knew what he was doing. But for an instant I couldn't give up control because I was used to making all the decisions. Now I had no choice. I had to hand the authority over to a complete stranger. I asked if we could call Dr. McQuaide, our excellent team doctor, to come over and perform the surgery. Finally I said, "May I speak to the anesthesiologist?"

"Be my guest," the doctor said and pointed down the hall to his office.

I walked into the anesthesiologist's office and saw a young dark-haired doctor sitting behind his desk, eating a sandwich. I stood across from him and spoke sternly, "I understand you're going to give my son, John Mark, some anesthesia." He put down his sandwich and looked up at me. "Well, he can't tolerate it. He's not supposed to have surgery," I said.

"We really don't have a choice," the young doctor said. "I will monitor him carefully."

I bent down and looked at him squarely in the eye. "I want you to handle this just exactly right. Don't you dare give him an ounce too much of that anesthesia. Make sure, though, that you give him enough, but just don't give him too much. Not an ounce too much." I got up to leave.

"You're putting pressure on me, aren't you?" asked the anesthesiologist as I walked toward the door.

"Yeah, I'm putting pressure on you," I said, turning and facing him. "I'm telling you it's got to be exactly right."

"Coach, you've got a football team and you do the best job you can to win, and I respect that." The doctor stood up and headed out the door. "Now, you've got to trust me to do my job to the best of my ability.

Dr. McQuaide came right over and I followed him as he headed down the hallway to where Johnny lay on the stretcher. The anesthesiologist then scooped Johnny up in his arms, leaving behind the bloodstained stretcher, and carried him down the hall. He was to be operated on immediately. I stood in the hall, holding on to Ruth Ann's arm, watching Johnny and the anesthesiologist disappear behind the heavy green doors to the operating room. A severe panic gripped me.

I sat down on the sofa in the waiting room and closed my eyes and for a minute I had a vision of Johnny's funeral. The service was being held in the Lamar Avenue Church of Christ in Paris and the congregation was singing Johnny's favorite hymn, "How Great Thou Art." After the preacher said a few words, Elmer Smith, Lee Cooper, and Bob Mullinex, acting as pallbearers, picked up the small white coffin and carried it out of the church, toward the grave. These men had been so kind and giving to Johnny and were really his best friends. There was an inscription on his tombstone that read, "He loved the farm on a beautiful day," because whenever we went for a long walk on the farm, Johnny would say to us, "Mom, Pop, I love the farm on a beautiful day." I was deep in a trance until I felt someone standing over me. It was a nurse asking me to fill out a series of medical forms for Johnny.

"Coach Stallings, our phone has been ringing off the hook," she said. "The hospital has had to put another telephone operator on duty to field all the calls we've been getting from folks inquiring about Johnny."

"Well, we did leave in the middle of church," I said. "I guess the word got out." It made me feel a little bit better knowing that there were a lot of people in College Station who were concerned about

Johnny. I methodically filled out the papers attached to the clipboard and walked back to the waiting room, where Ruth Ann sat nervously leafing through magazines. I put my arms around her and she started to cry. I looked up and saw Dr. McQuaide walking toward us.

"Success!" He smiled broadly. "Johnny is fine. He will have to stay here a few nights because we need to keep an eye on him. It wasn't glass after all but a Meckel's diverticulum, which is just like a little projection the size of your finger that grows right on the intestine. It's sort of a ballooning out but long, and then when the end of it wears through where food gets caught in there, it starts bleeding."

The anesthesiologist came over and shook my hand. "He handled the anesthesia like a pro," he said. My whole body felt lighter and I gave him a hearty handshake and thanked him a million times.

Later that night the anesthesiologist came into the room where Johnny, Ruth Ann, and I slept. I watched from my cot, ten feet from Johnny's bed, as the doctor smoothed Johnny's forehead with the back of his hand and sat down in a straight-backed chair right next to his bed. Ruth Ann and I dozed fitfully and I kept opening my eyes, looking at that chair next to Johnny's bed and expecting it to be empty. But there sat the doctor, straight up, holding Johnny's little hand, making sure that the IV line wasn't getting tangled up when he tossed and turned and watching him intently as he slept. When the sunlight came streaming through the blinds the next morning, I saw the doctor tiptoe out of the room.

Ruth Ann and I stayed in the hospital for three more nights, only going home for brief periods to change our clothes and bathe. Johnny was weak and pale and he slept most of those days. Even though the doctors kept reassuring us that he would be fine, we couldn't leave him alone for a minute. I bombarded the doctors with questions about what he should eat and how much he should sleep. I was terrified that this could happen again, and more than anything I wanted the doctors to offer their reassurance that it wouldn't. By the time we left the hospital with Johnny he was back to his old self, just a little bit more tired.

Back at work I had a difficult time concentrating. As we continued losing games I kept reliving the sudden terror at church as I saw the blood pouring from Johnny. I couldn't stop thinking of the trauma at the hospital, watching as they took him into the operating room and believing that he would never survive his ordeal. Although we ended up with a bleak 2–9 season, I wasn't as upset as I might have been. I found myself reflecting a little more and putting things into perspective. After all, my son had almost died that fall.

The 1971 season didn't start out any better. We had won only our first game and had lost the next five. One Friday afternoon as I gathered the players together in the locker room before our next game, against Baylor, I suddenly found myself describing Johnny's ordeal. I had never talked about him to my players, but now I was saying, "He's a fighter. He's made it against the odds and you can, too. He was told he wouldn't survive, but he fought and he did." The players were especially quiet after I spoke, and we went on to win the game against Baylor by one point — the final score was 10–9. Then we beat Arkansas, SMU, and Rice. At times I wondered if Johnny's near-death experience hadn't motivated me over the last year to coach better than ever. I felt a new kind of intensity and determination, and I wanted the players to go out there and fight as if there were no tomorrow. We were turning things around, beating teams that we hadn't defeated in years.

There was a great deal riding on our final game of the season. If we beat the University of Texas we were going to get an invitation to the Liberty Bowl. I was so nervous that I got sick to my stomach right before the game. But, we lost badly — 34–14. I was upset and disappointed, just as I was any time we lost, but I viewed it as a temporary failure. I went over the good wins we'd had over the season and I felt better. So when the phone rang that cold November night and I learned that the board of trustees wanted to see me, I thought that they were probably going to give me a raise. I put on a clean shirt and headed over to the president's house, where the board and the president were to meet me. I walked in, just as confident as I could be that I was going to get a raise. I looked around the room at the entire board and then at the president and saw that their faces were solemn. I was a little puzzled by the stern way in which they asked me to sit down. I sat across from Pete Peterson.

Our eyes locked and finally Pete spoke up, "I'm sorry, Bebes. We've got some rather bad news. We are going to have to replace you." My face felt hot and I started to sweat. I was so embarrassed and devastated that I couldn't speak. I looked at him, but I really couldn't see him. I must have sat there for a good minute staring into space.

"I'm fired?" I finally mustered the courage to ask. The board members solemnly nodded their heads in unison. "But I have another year left on my contract." The board said they'd pay me, but that really wasn't the point. A contract is a contract — period. I'd had other coaching opportunities offered to me after we won the SWC title in 1967, but I turned them down because I felt I had a contract to fulfill. It wasn't the money I wanted, it was the job. I thought a school administration should judge what you did by what you had done, then tell you what you had to do to stay.

"It really doesn't come down to how many games we had to win last year," the president finally spoke up. "The point is that we have to be competitive in the conference."

"Well, if Arkansas didn't kick a long field goal against Rice, we'd still be in the thick of it," I said. "And, if we had won the last game, we'd have gone to the Liberty Bowl. I call that being competitive, and I have the best team coming up that I've ever had."

There was nothing else I could say. It was obvious that the scoreboard had won. The president just sat there shaking his head, saying he was sorry. I felt like I had been doing a fine job and I was proud of the way I had run the program. I had tried to give my players something to help them grow up a little. We had excellent facilities, good attendance at the games, and a first-rate staff. Sure, the scoreboard is what really counted, but everyone knew that recruiting at A&M was difficult, and I believed that my handling of the players and situations was to the very best of my ability. Didn't the board think that those qualities should have counted for something? Everyone knew that by the early seventies it had become all but impossible to recruit. Now all of a sudden I was fired from the place I had gone to school, where we had won the Southwest Conference championship and the Cotton Bowl. I felt completely defeated and I started wondering what I could have possibly done to change things. I wanted to pack up and leave College Station just as soon as I could.

We sold the house immediately and on the same day I sold my stock and resigned as a director of the A&M bank. We moved back to Paris to live with Mammy and put our furniture in storage nearby. Now here I was without direction and too depressed for any kind of constructive thinking. Coaching was in my blood and I loved associating with the other coaches and players. I had spent the last fourteen years of my life doing something I was passionate about and now I wondered if I'd ever have that chance again.

I had no idea how important the farm would become almost right away. It was my salvation as well as my escape. Every morning I'd get up early, pull on a pair of blue jeans and a work shirt, and head out there just as the sun was coming up. Then I would get out my chain saw and cut down some bois d'arc trees. There were a lot of those thorny, tough trees on the farm and they were good for making fences and posts. They were hard on a chain saw and tough to chop, but hacking away at them seemed to get my frustrations out. I desperately needed to create something, something that lasted, and I began to build a large fence to keep the cattle in. I wanted the phone to ring during the day. I wanted to have job offers, but I knew that I couldn't just sit around and wait for that to happen, and I was much too defeated to pick up the phone myself and start making calls about possible jobs.

I needed to be alone. I'd chop for a while and then I'd think back to getting that phone call and then sitting in that tense meeting at the college president's house. Over and over I saw each of the eight faces of the board of trustees as they shook my hand and wished me well when I left, and then I'd get furious all over again. I thought we had played our last game, against Texas, pretty well. No question that we had fumbled that punt, and then the game just started snowballing in the opposite direction. I replayed that game so many times in my mind that I got a headache. In fact, I'd spend the entire day thinking about how we could have possibly won it.

I was concerned about my whole family but especially Johnny, and every time I thought about him getting sick I'd pick up my ax and chop down a tree. For the first time ever we didn't have any health insurance, and I'd start remembering what happened to Johnny while we were in church and I'd have to stop myself. I couldn't imagine what we'd possibly do if he became really ill again.

When I got home at night Ruth Ann and I would spend hours talking about the possibility that I'd quit football altogether and we'd become ranchers and raise cattle. The land meant more and more to me every day, and I thought that this might be a good time to start looking at spots to clear so that we could build a modest house on the farm. We had been steadily adding to our herd of cattle and had acquired some Hereford bulls and some crossbreeds. Gradually we bought a few horses and frequently started to day-dream about the good life and how we could make a living on our land. It might be a big relief, we thought, to be out from under the constant pressures of a football coach. Maybe, we said to ourselves, we'd finally be able to find a place nearby for Johnny to get some good schooling. He hadn't made any kind of academic or social progress in the two-day-a-week program in Bryan, and I was concerned that now all he was doing was basically existing.

I found myself being extra sensitive around the girls when I got home. It was tough on them to move abruptly during the school year. Jackie had been learning how to add and subtract and her reading was getting better each day. Now she had to start in a new school, and Anna Lee and Laurie had to leave their junior high. Those school years were difficult enough for young people, with dating and cliques forming. They had heard their friends at school in College Station whispering and laughing in the hallways that their daddy had gotten fired. I knew they felt upset about that. But Johnny was a comfort; it just wasn't a big deal to him that I didn't have a job. In fact, he was happy to spend time with me, so some days I'd bring him out to the farm and instead of working we'd ride on the tractor together through the barren fields, the wind at our faces.

The winter of 1972 was a cold one, maybe the coldest Paris ever had. In fact, one frigid January morning I tried to leave the house from Mammy's back door, pushing and pulling on the door, but it wouldn't budge. It was frozen shut and we couldn't get it open for three or four days. Somehow, when you are sad and depressed it always seems colder.

CHAPTER 6

DISCOVERING THE PROS

B Y the end of January, the cold snap had let up and out at the farm the ground was soft and muddy. The warmer weather allowed me to get more done and I started staying out there later, working alongside Mr. Henry — branding cattle, replacing worn shingles on the roof of the cabin, building fences, and cleaning out the stables. He knew how to fix just about anything and he'd entertain me with his stories about hoop snakes, coach whips, and old Indian mounds. I heard the story of how he held a horse by the tail as they crossed the creeks after the bottoms overflowed so many times that I could recite it word for word. After we had worked for a while he'd say, "Boy, I've got to cool," which of course meant we both sat down to rest. It seemed like we talked more than we worked, but it was good therapy for me.

One evening when I returned to Mammy's, Ruth Ann greeted me with some good news. "You had a telephone call today from Bill Peterson." Bill was the head coach of the Houston Oilers. I first met him when he was coaching at Florida State, and later we developed a good relationship when he was the head coach at Rice University.

"He said he wanted to talk to you. He'll be calling tomorrow around two o'clock," Ruth Ann said. For the first time in months I felt optimistic, even a little excited. Maybe something good was finally going to happen. The next morning I decided not to go to the farm. I wanted to make sure I would be there when he called. While Ruth Ann and I ate lunch that afternoon, I couldn't stop looking at my watch. At 1:45, I was pacing the floor waiting for his call. The chimes on Mammy's grandfather clock rang twice and I sat in the chair by the phone and rested my hand on the receiver. Two o'clock came and went and then it was 2:05 and then 2:10 and then 2:15. The ticking of the clock seemed to grow louder now and I stared at the brass chime as it swung back and forth.

I turned the television on and flipped through the stations, turned it off, and sat in the silent room for another ten minutes — looking through a pile of old newspapers and magazines and staring at the clock. Its single bong announcing 2:30 made me jump and I got up and paced around the room. Finally at 2:45 it was obvious he wasn't going to call, so I decided to drive out to the farm.

Late that night when I returned Ruth Ann said that Bill had called at the end of the afternoon and that he would try to call back sometime the next day.

I debated whether to stay home that morning and wait for his call and finally I thought that I'd be pretty upset if I missed it. I ate breakfast, read the paper, sat by the phone, watched television, and when I took the trash out, I moved the phone as close to the back door as I could so I wouldn't miss the ringing. No call. After a late lunch, I went back into the living room, paced up and down, and stared out the window. The sky had turned a dark gray, and pretty soon I heard thunder and saw bolts of lightning flash across the sky.

The rain quickly started and I ran around the house, closing windows and doors.

When I went back into the living room, I picked up the phone, and my suspicions were confirmed. No dial tone. The storm had knocked out the phone line. It wasn't restored until the next morning.

Finally a few evenings later he called and we arranged that I would meet with him in Houston, but his tone of voice was not particularly encouraging. Nevertheless I was pleased that we had set up a meeting. I flew to Houston, but as I sat in his office, there was no real substance to his questions and I sensed that we were having a courtesy interview. A few days later I picked up the *Dallas Morning News* and saw that he had hired someone else.

A couple of weeks after that, I received a call from Fran Curci, the head coach at the University of Miami, asking me if I would be interested in the defensive coordinator position there. He was an outstanding offensive coach but had little defensive experience. He told me that I had the qualifications and expertise he was looking for. I felt the interview went extremely well, and when I called Ruth Ann that night from Miami to tell her about it, she told me that Coach Tom Landry had called from the Dallas Cowboys. Early the next morning I called him, but he was out of the office for a few days. His secretary, Marge Kelly, said Tom wanted to talk to me about joining his staff. She scheduled a meeting for us and one week later I met with him and he offered me the job coaching the defensive secondary. Once again, Coach Bryant had gone to bat for me by contacting Landry and saying: "We've got a coach who's fixing to get out of coaching and we don't want to lose that kind of person. We need coaches like Gene Stallings."

As happy as I was about getting the job with the Cowboys, if I'd had my druthers I would have preferred still to be the head coach at A&M. I knew nothing about professional ball: I'd never coached or played pro ball. In fact, I'd never even been to a professional football game. For the last seven years I'd had a staff of eight full-time coaches working for me. Gradually they'd begun to accept Johnny. Of course, they really didn't have a whole lot of choice in the matter because I was their boss. But despite what they might have felt deep inside, their outward approval put me at ease. I would be coming from a place where I had total control to a place where I would be just one more coach. But, I had to put my concerns about my new job behind me — quickly. After all, I was lucky.

I knew Coach Landry only by his reputation and it was bigger than big. Just two weeks earlier, on January 16, 1972, the Cowboys had beaten the Miami Dolphins — to win the Super Bowl for the first time. Tom had grown up in a small Texas town and had played high school football, just as I had. He later went to the University of Texas and became an outstanding fullback, and after graduating he played for the New York Giants as a cornerback, eventually becoming a player-coach and later a full-time member of the Giants staff. He was the first coach the Cowboys ever had and he had the reputation of being fair, honest, and straight as an arrow — if he said "dad gum" he considered that cussing. Unlike Coach Bryant, who had loads of magnetism and charm and was a genius at making you feel like you could beat just about anybody, Coach Landry's public persona was that of a cold, businesslike man who rarely showed emotion. He made things happen because he took special care with every detail. He was a perfectionist and an expert tactician and considered by many to be the best coach in the NFL.

Before long, it was time to move. Ruth Ann and I looked out the bedroom window of Mammy's house as the moving men lifted our furniture out of the large storage van and transferred it into an orange and white Allied moving van. The children looked sad as they stood at the end of the driveway and watched the men struggle up the ramp with our kitchen table, the last piece of furniture to be loaded. Here we were disrupting them in the middle of a school year for the second time in three months! They were just getting used to their schools in Paris, and of course, Johnny had never been happier, living at Mammy's house and loving the constant attention from her.

After every last suitcase was secured on the top of the car, and the moving van was packed so high that the men had trouble latching the door, we all hugged and kissed Mammy for the jillionth time and piled into our station wagon. She stood on her porch, her long apron stained from baking brownies for our trip, and waved goodbye. It was an especially emotional time for us because right before we left Mammy told us that she had been diagnosed with Parkinson's disease. But whenever we asked her about her illness and how she was feeling, she changed the subject. She was of the generation that said you didn't talk about yourself when you felt bad. But in the last few months I had noticed a slight tremor in her hands as she folded laundry or held a book while she read to Johnny. And sometimes when I'd come home from the farm in the middle of the day, I'd find her napping, which was unusual for her. Now, we were driving off from her house on a blustery Saturday in April and heading through town, over the railroad tracks and south, to the big city of Dallas.

Those were the days before seat belt laws, and Martha Kate took Johnny's place in the flimsy little car seat that hooked on to the front seat. She sat in the middle, between Ruth Ann and me, while the three older girls and Johnny bounced around on one another's laps in the backseat. General and our two cats took up the entire empty space in the rear of the car that we referred to as the "way back." As we drove south on Highway 19 toward Commerce, I glanced in the rearview mirror and noticed that Johnny was crying and murmuring, "Mammy, Mammy." The girls put their arms around him, trying in vain to comfort him, and I could tell that they were just as sad as Johnny about leaving Mammy behind.

"It's okay, Johnny, you'll see Mammy, soon." Anna Lee held his hand and patted his back. "Johnny, it's okay."

But his crying turned into a loud wail. The girls sat there silently until I heard Laurie, Jackie, and Anna Lee call out, "Johnny, Johnny! I bet you can read that sign." They pointed to a large white sign with bold black lettering marking the entrance to a gas station. Johnny sat up straight as an arrow, rubbed his eyes, and read, "GAS." Squeals of delight filled the backseat of the car and I glanced back in the mirror again to see all of the girls patting him. As we headed up the road, a little farther, we came to another sign. "What does that sign over there say, Johnny?" The girls were getting more excited.

Johnny answered, "65 M-P-H," and grinned. We came upon a few more signs, some Johnny knew, others he didn't. Soon we stopped for gas and some Cokes. I watched Johnny carefully as he walked toward the restrooms. He was going to be ten years old in a couple of months, yet he was only as tall as most five-year-olds. Dressed in blue jeans that were rolled up several times at the ankle and a light blue T-shirt exposing his bony arms, Johnny looked frail, almost breakable. He paused before opening the restroom door, and then, looking proudly back at me, he smiled and in a loud voice read, "MEN." I clapped my hands and gave him a thumbs-up sign. Then I turned to Ruth Ann, took her arm, and whispered, "When in the world did Johnny learn to read?"

"He's been learning for the last few weeks at Mrs. Cunning-ham's," she said. "The girls have been anxious for you to notice."

"Well, why didn't you tell me?" I asked.

"You just had to see for yourself."

In just three weeks at Mrs. Cunningham's school in Paris, Johnny had learned to read at least ten words, and he could recognize just as many numbers. Now it hit me like a ton of bricks how preoccupied I had been in those months after getting fired. I had been so self-absorbed that I hadn't realized how much my son was learning there.

Of course, I had been excited that cold afternoon in January when Ruth Ann and Johnny had come out to the farm and called to me while I hammered shingles to the cabin roof. "Bebes! Good news. We've got a school for Johnny. I think it's going to be great!" Ruth Ann explained that when Mrs. Cunningham had heard that we were in town, she called to invite Johnny to her school. Later that day, we drove over to a small wooden building that was on the same grounds as Jackie's elementary school. I remembered as we walked through the school's front door how impressed I was by the large colorful mural that covered the hallway wall that faced us. Mrs. Cunningham had come out from her classroom and greeted us warmly, taking Johnny's hand. I recognized her as the kind and friendly mother of our close friend in high school, Emma Lee, and the wife of our high school principal. She still looked the same as she did when we knew her over twenty years before — petite and neatly dressed, but now at sixty her hair was silver and she had it neatly pulled back in a small bun. As we walked into her classroom I had asked Mrs. Cunningham about the mural. She proudly told me that the children at her school had recently painted it.

She showed us a kiln in the corner of the classroom and I had watched, fascinated, as her eight students carefully molded clay into various shapes and then placed them in the small oven for firing. I'd never seen anyone fire and glaze clay and I was amazed by the skillful way the children changed the big mounds of gray clay into dogs, cats, dishes, and human shapes. I thought back to how Johnny would come home with little "Dick and Jane" primers and how the girls would curl up on Mammy's sofa with him after dinner at night and get him to read.

And now, as Ruth Ann and I stood waiting for Johnny to come out of the gas station's restroom, I realized what a major breakthrough this was for us. Although Ruth Ann had been seeing his progress at Mrs. Cunningham's for weeks, I now understood, after hearing him read the signs, that he was truly capable of learning things in school. I rubbed the palms of my hands together and felt the calluses I had developed from working on the farm. Looking back on the last few months since the sudden firing from A&M, I now felt ashamed of my behavior.

I had been in a dense fog, still hurting from the rejection. Night after night, I'd come home after being at the farm all day, and the first thing I'd do would be to ask Ruth Ann if anyone had called for me. Her usual reply — "No, not today, Bebes. But I just know you are going to get some calls soon" — always hit me hard, and seeing the concerned look on her face made me feel even more depressed. She was trying hard to be brave and strong and I knew I should try too, but I just couldn't think straight. I couldn't even initiate my own calls about potential jobs.

At the dinner table I rarely talked, barely focusing on the family's conversation around me. I'd eat quickly and excuse myself, turn the television on to watch football games, as I thought about what my next step would be. I'd go over and over in my mind how it had all fallen apart and how I had failed. I had wasted so much time being upset that I hadn't even noticed my son's progress in school. Although Ruth Ann had often told me what a gifted teacher Mrs. Cunningham was, and how well Johnny was doing there, I wasn't really hearing anything except the constant voice inside my head, examining each day of my seven years as head coach at A&M and wondering how I could have possibly gotten fired from my alma mater.

During the short time that Johnny had been in Mrs. Cunningham's school, she had done more for his education than anybody else. Not only was she a warm and compassionate teacher but she also knew what was going on with special education programs around the country, and when Ruth Ann told her that we were moving to Dallas she told us that the Richardson school district there was way ahead of other districts in the area in teaching children with special needs.

The year was 1972 and the Education for All Handicapped Children Act, the federal law declaring that every child has a right to a public school education, no matter what the disability, was still three years away from being passed. But all during the 1960s and early seventies laws had been enacted to ensure the educational rights of children with disabilities. Some states had already guaranteed that children with disabilities would be entitled to a free appropriate education in the least restrictive environment. But Texas was not one of them. At the time, most services for children with disabilities were provided through private schools and social service agencies like United Cerebral Palsy and the Association for Retarded Citizens. But some parents and teachers who were ahead of their time knew that children with disabilities could be taught successfully. And now, in a few Texas communities, special education classes had started to spring up.

The day after Coach Landry offered me the job, Ruth Ann and I had driven to Dallas for two days to look for a house. We had one goal in mind: we had to live in the Richardson school district. We bought the second house we saw, a one-floor, U-shaped taupe-colored house with four bedrooms, on Ferndale Avenue. We couldn't wait to visit the children's schools — especially Johnny's. Jackie's school, Wallace Elementary, was right across the street from our new house. But since there were no special education classes housed in that school, Johnny had to go six blocks away to Lake Highlands Elementary School, where children with disabilities were bused in from all over the district.

Nancy Hall, who would be Johnny's teacher, invited us to spend some time observing the cheerful-looking classroom. The twenty-

115

five or so children had various disabilities — some were in wheel-chairs, some wore braces, a few had Down syndrome, and it was hard to say what the disability was with some of the others. For the short time we were there, the noise level was nerve-racking, yet Nancy seemed energetic as she moved around the classroom from one student to the next, smiling and praising each of them.

It was hard for me to believe that Johnny would finally be going to a real school from eight-thirty to two-thirty — Monday through Friday — just like the other children, and I was eager and anxious for him to do well there, although I had no idea what he was capable of learning. I could only imagine the relief that Ruth Ann must have felt knowing that finally he would be in expert hands where he would be safe and have the chance to develop his abilities.

But as we left Johnny's new school that day, I wondered how in the world he was going to make himself understood in such a noisy classroom. His speech still wasn't very clear and people often struggled to understand him. I pictured him raising his hand, trying to answer a question, only to have his teacher ask him to repeat himself. I could see him getting frustrated and not participating. After all, his classes were now going to be a lot bigger than anything he was used to, and I was sure that the teacher wouldn't have a lot of time to devote to him.

When he was younger, his inability to communicate well verbally had created huge barriers between him and others, and I thought back with sadness to all the times adults, including Ruth Ann and me, had asked him to repeat himself. I could distinctly remember different children's voices as I overheard them tease Johnny and say that he couldn't talk right. No longer did he cry and scream as he had done as a very young child so that he would be understood. Instead he'd end up impersonating someone until we finally understood who he was talking about, or he would act out his intention until we figured out that he wanted to eat, run, or sleep.

If we still didn't understand he would eventually simply shut down, just like when he was little, unable to communicate, isolated in a world of his own. And though now at nearly ten years of age he could identify so many things, he used short, clipped sentences. In fact, his speech had a sort of stripped-down quality to it. For instance, if he saw a Raggedy Ann doll, he might end up saying something like "girl." But his vocabulary was steadily growing and I was convinced that this was because the girls talked to him so often and because from an early age Ruth Ann had introduced him to the world of music and singing. Johnny had difficulty pronouncing all the words to the different songs he knew, but he could carry a tune really well. It was easy to recognize the song because he could sing the melody. But even though he had made tremendous progress with his language over the last few years, to the point where people were beginning to understand him a good deal of the time, I was still concerned about how he'd relate to his classmates and teachers.

Mrs. Cunningham had been the first person to tell us that many children with Down syndrome have a lot of trouble speaking in a way that can be understood by others. She explained to us that Johnny, like many other children with Down's, had low muscle tone and a smaller mouth than other children, which affected his ability to form sounds correctly and clearly. Although his tongue was a normal size, it appeared to be larger because of his smaller mouth. For the first time I understood that it was probably easier for him to use the letter "w" for the "el" sound. He'd say "wemon" for "lemon" or "wittle" for "little." And for the first time I understood why he called spaghetti, "pasghetti." Mrs. Cunningham referred to mixing up these kinds of words as sequencing difficulties.

Yet, I reasoned, Johnny's ability to understand language better than he could express it might serve him well. Just before we left College Station, I had started to see a sociable side to him that I had never noticed before. When he'd be in a room and somebody new would come in, he'd go right up to that person and start making introductions. I could tell that he had a keen intuition about people, and he always knew when Pop was tired or when one of the girls was upset over something that happened at school. He liked to comfort us and he could see how pleased we were with his hugs and kisses. Maybe he'd attract the teacher with this warm and loving personality. I could only hope so.

As we pulled into the steep driveway of our new home at 10031 Ferndale Avenue and watched the moving van in front of us slowly and carefully wind its way down, Jackie quickly pointed out to Johnny how great the driveway would be for riding down in their moon wagon. They started scheming about how they would be able to get their wagon from the loaded moving van and take a spin down the sloping blacktop. We had bought the house so hurriedly that I hadn't even noticed that it was quite far below street level, or the steep grade of the driveway, and how much busier Ferndale Avenue was than any of the streets we had ever lived on. It seemed like a car whizzed by every two minutes on the two-lane street, and it was so much noisier than our quiet street in Bryan.

When the children saw our new house, they ran inside and inspected every room, each trying to claim the biggest bedroom. Ruth Ann and I stood out front and admired the beautiful pink and red roses across the front of the house which had just burst into bloom. Red brick steps ran from the street down to the house. Our new neighborhood, Lake Highlands, had been developed in the early 1960s, and was mostly one-story brick houses, like ours. It had a suburban feel to it, yet I had noticed as we drove through the neighborhood that there were still open, undeveloped fields surrounding our area, which made me feel a little more at home.

The movers unpacked the van, and Ruth Ann, the children, and I unloaded the car. But that's as far as we got. Boxes were piled upon boxes in the living room and the front hall, and the furniture sat in the middle of the rooms. But we were anxious to explore and left everything just where it was and started out for a walk. The first thing that the children noticed was a playground almost directly across the street. We went over and let them swing for a while, pleased to see so many children in the neighborhood who seemed to be about their ages. I carried Martha Kate on my shoulders and the other children ran ahead, and as we walked down Ferndale, I felt like we had landed in a very big town.

Our first stop was the brand-new neighborhood library, and the older girls ran inside with Johnny tagging along right behind them and quickly got lost in the stacks while Ruth Ann, Martha Kate, and I wandered in and sat in large comfortable chairs. We were surprised when we looked out the large windows and saw cows grazing across the street in a large pasture!

Down the street we came upon the high school where Anna Lee would go. The children scattered, peering in the windows of the empty school and skipping around the basketball court and the football field. We did the same thing at Laurie's junior high, and at Jackie's school. But we made an extra big fuss about Johnny's school when we got there and I noticed how pleased and proud he seemed about his very own new school.

Monday morning rolled around quickly and we all woke much earlier than usual. The children ran around the house, looking for the right clothes to wear, and they dug into boxes for notebooks, pens, and rulers. At the breakfast table they ate fast and barely spoke, and I could tell that they were apprehensive but excited about starting a new school, just as I was about beginning my new job with the pros.

That morning when I set out for work I had to pinch myself that I was actually going to my job at the Cowboys. They had fans everywhere. Unlike, say, the Cleveland Browns, who performed primarily for the people who lived in northeastern Ohio, or the Oakland Raiders, who performed for the people who lived in Oakland and the Bay Area, the Cowboys had a national following.

They were innovators and one of the first teams to use the computer to scout and to catalog players' strengths and weaknesses. The Cowboys were one of the first teams to use offensively what they called multiple sets, which meant using lots of different formations and personnel. Tom Landry invented a defense called the "flex" that the Cowboys were the only team in the league to use. He claimed it was based on engineering principles, with each player responsible for his assigned area or "gap," except for the middle linebacker, who was responsible for two gaps.

Most other professional teams were constantly changing general managers and head coaches, but the Cowboys held on to the same personnel since joining the NFL in 1961. Clint Murchison Jr., the team's owner, let Tom Landry and Tex Schramm, the president of the Cowboys, run the team. Tex was a flamboyant guy, a real promoter, who injected a kind of Hollywood glamour into the organization. He had come up through the ranks in public relations, and had been the director of PR for the Los Angeles Rams. He knew what the crowd wanted and how to fill a stadium. He took the sideline cheerleaders, outfitted them in flashy blue and white uniforms, and turned them into a squad of accomplished dancers. He even hired a choreographer for halftime shows. The fans were almost as anxious now to have the cheerleaders' autographs as the players'.

The Cowboys were a sharp-looking organization and the players' uniforms still look great today — white uniforms with blue lettering for home games and blue uniforms with white lettering for away games. The team's signature blue star on a silver background was recognizable anywhere in America as the Cowboys' helmet logo.

It didn't take me long to figure out that pro football was big

As the twenty-nine-year old head coach at Texas A&M, more than anything, I wanted to win games, but recruiting was difficult during the Vietnam War years.
(Courtesy Texas A&M Sports Information)

I was the pupil playing the teacher — the best of em all — Coach Bryant, the 1968 Cotton Bowl. Our team (Texas A&M) beat his (Alabama) 20–16. Coach Bryant was so pleased for me afterward that he lifted me up in the air when I went over to shake hands with him.
(Courtesy *Birmingham News*)

Johnny with his sisters (*clockwise from left*), Laurie, Anna Lee, and Jackie. At six, he was very small for his age and looked about three years younger. Jackie, at four years old, towered over him.
(Courtesy Ruth Ann Stallings)

College Station, 197
Johnny with anoth
new sister, Martha K
Clockwise from left
Johnny, Laurie, Ru
Ann, Martha Kate, n
Anna Lee, Jackie.
(Courtesy Ruth Ann Stalli

At a small birthday party for Mammy before we left for Dallas in 1972. Johnny, age nine, as always by Mammy's side.
(Courtesy Ruth Ann Stallings)

Johnny's looks began to change when he became a teenager.
(From the author's collection)

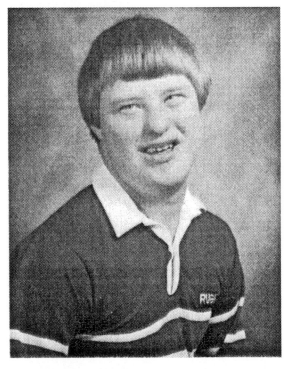

Johnny was the ring bearer at Anna Lee's wedding in May 1980. *Left to right:* Laurie, Johnny, Anna Lee, Martha Kate, and Jackie.
(Courtesy Joseph L. Pilliod)

Summer 1987. At the farm near St. Louis filming the United Way commercial. Johnny liked being a "movie star" for a day.
(Courtesy VITA: M. Pellegrini)

In March of 1993, after winning the national championship, the team was invited to Washington, D.C., and spent an hour with President Clinton. We presented him with a crimson jersey. Johnny told the President that his daddy coached the number one team.
(Courtesy Kent Gidley)

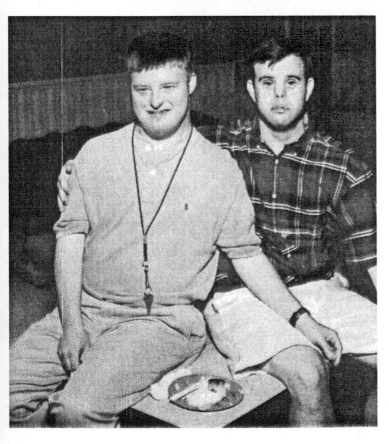

Johnny and his best friend, Bradley Block, relaxing after a birthday party in 1993.
(Courtesy University of Alabama)

At the RISE dedication in February 1995. Ruth Ann and I, Betty Shirley, and Martha Cook are shown with some of Johnny's friends who work at RISE through the Betty Shirley Employment Program. They are (*left to right*) Yancy Christian, Bradley Block, Traci Green, Gina Noland, Johnny, and Kevin Kendrick.
(Courtesy University of Alabama)

John Mark had a few words to say to the crowd at the RISE dedication as proud Pop looked on.
(Courtesy University of Alabama)

Johnny spent as much time at the RISE center as he could. He loved playing with the children and helping Dr. Martha Cook, the director, shown here
(Courtesy University of Alabama)

Alabama's 1996 team — and an honorary member, John Mark.
(Courtesy Kent Gidley)

Johnny was ecstatic when Alabama beat Auburn 24–23 in 1996. His sisters
Martha Kate and Laurie shared his enthusiasm and so did his nephew John
Mark. Right after the game I announced I was leaving as head coach of the
University of Alabama, and Johnny broke into tears.
(Courtesy Ron Harris/*Daily Mountain Eagle*)

Johnny with Kareem McNeal and Santa Claus at the RISE Center in 1996.
(Courtesy University of Alabama)

Johnny thanking t
crowd for coming
his farewell party
the Paul Bryant
Conference Cente
January 1997.
(Courtesy Robert Sutto

business. In college, the youngsters were supposed to come to get an education first. But with the Cowboys football was a livelihood. Unlike college players, they were all different ages and had a variety of life experiences; some were even older than the coaches.

On my first day at practice as the secondary coach I was all fired up, full of the kind of energy and excitement that I had always used to motivate my players. I was used to taking the college players and building up a sort of frenzy each week so that they would play hard on Saturdays. I walked into the first meeting and there sat Cowboy greats, among them Mel Renfro, Herb Adderly, Charlie Waters, and Cliff Harris. I shook hands with each of the players, and then I started the meeting by saying, "Now, I want you all to know that I'm looking for some enthusiasm."

The players all kind of snickered and looked at each other.

"And, I want to see some hitting," I continued. Again, the players looked at one another, rolled their eyes, and then glanced back at me with an uncomprehending look on their faces.

Then I announced that we were going to have some tackling drills. Mel put his hand up and said, "Uh, Coach, we don't do that here in the NFL."

I felt my face turning red. I bit my tongue a little, but I was getting kind of worked up. Here was a player challenging me! In college the coaches were always right. I could tell that the players sensed that I was upset. Finally, Cliff Harris stepped forward and tried to explain how they never did tackling drills. I was stunned to hear the players talk to me like this, but finally we worked out a compromise and they ended up doing a shortened version for me.

The next day while I was in the locker room, I noticed that Bob Lilly, a six-five, 255-pound defensive lineman who had started playing when the team was formed in 1961, was sitting on the bench puffing on a cigar. I walked over to him and said, "Bob, what are you doing smoking that cigar?" He pulled the cigar out of his mouth and gave me a puzzled look, and right then I knew that I was in a different league, no longer in the college ranks. I was now coaching professionals, who had a different set of rules. They were mature men playing a tough game for high stakes.

Coach Landry was very patient with me. In his statement to the press when I was first hired, he praised my abilities as a coach, saying that he knew I'd be able to make the adjustment to the pros easily and do a good job for the Cowboys just as Jim Myers, the offensive line coach and running game coordinator, had. Jim had also been fired from A&M before Hank Foldberg, my predecessor, was hired.

I spent a lot of time studying playbooks and game films and talking to other coaches, trying to learn as much as I could as fast as possible. When I was coaching at A&M, even-numbered plays always went to the right, but now in Dallas they went to the left. The terminology was so much different — in college when I had talked about forces, they were "sky" and "cloud," and now all of a sudden they were "rifle" and "pistol." They meant the same thing, but now I was introduced to a whole new set of phrases. There were more games and details in the pros than in college, and I spent hours analyzing the opponents until I couldn't see straight any-more.

I was trying to form opinions on some of the guys like Charlie Waters, Cliff Harris, Benny Barnes, and Mark Washington. They were all fine young players, and I liked their competitive spirit and the way they put their hearts into practicing. Most of all I liked the way they played to win. Yet I was not sure how Coach Landry wanted me to coach them.

I was getting home each night later and later, and many nights the children had already gone to bed by the time I walked in the door. I missed our family dinners, which I had always looked for-ward to. Now instead of hearing about everybody's day at the dinner table I relied on Ruth Ann to tell me what was going on in the children's lives — how they were getting along in their schools, if they were making friends and liking Dallas. It seemed like she and the children were adjusting well to their new environs. Now with Johnny going to school, she had more free time, and she hired a baby-sitter named May Allen to help with Martha Kate.

Johnny was always the first one up and dressed every morning, waking his sisters and then us. We tried to sit down together and have breakfast as a family so I could at least see the children for a little while. I noticed that Johnny couldn't wait to get to school in the mornings.

One Saturday morning, a few weeks after we had arrived in Dallas, we had all slept in a little later than usual and we were sitting at the breakfast table when one of the children asked, "Where's Johnny?" Ruth Ann and the girls were planning to spend the day unpacking the rest of the boxes and organizing their rooms and I was headed out to a meeting.

"I just saw him, wasn't he outside with General?" I asked as I grabbed my jacket to leave. I had seen Johnny very briefly before breakfast. He had been wearing a pair of red pajamas given to him the past Christmas by Bob Mullinex, and he and General had been roughhousing in his bedroom.

Now I noticed that the back door was wide open. I looked out the door and saw that General was not in the fenced-in backyard. I threw my jacket down and ran to Johnny's bedroom.

"Johnny wonny!" I called, using my nickname for him. I slowly tiptoed into his room, expecting him to play a trick on me and jump out from behind one of the unpacked cardboard boxes against his bedroom wall. Then I peeked behind the boxes. No Johnny. There were still times when he hid from me or simply disappeared, and now I felt guilty for not having put a lock on his door the minute we moved in. But I was sure that he was somewhere in his room, hiding, pulling a gag on Pop. Maybe he didn't want me to leave the house. I yanked open his closet door, envisioning General and Johnny huddled up together amid his shoes and clothes. Not there.

I ran outside to the front lawn, where Ruth Ann and the girls were gathered. Together we called out for General and then for Johnny, our voices growing louder and more frantic with every shout. But when we stopped to catch our breath there was total silence except for the distant buzz of a neighbor's lawn mower.

We had always lived in small towns and we weren't used to metropolitan areas and traffic. Just a few short blocks from our house, there were plenty of busy streets. I thought about the network of freeways linking Dallas with the suburbs that I drove on every day to work, and I had rash thoughts of Johnny walking along the side of those roadways. A child and dog wandering around alone on our street, Ferndale, was enough to make me worry. "Why don't we scatter?" I finally said to Ruth Ann and the girls.

"Bebes," Ruth Ann said, "I think we'd better call the police." I ran back inside, dialed the police, and reported Johnny and the dog missing. Back outside, we all ran in different directions. All of the backyards in Dallas had high fences around them and the alleyways behind the backyards led into people's garages. I hadn't met any of our neighbors yet, but now I found myself knocking on their doors, quickly introducing myself, and desperately asking if any of them had seen a ten-year-old boy wearing red pajamas. They all shook their heads.

"How about a large German shepherd?" I asked. Again, no one had seen them.

By this time I was distraught. My hands were beginning to shake and I started to sweat profusely. "Johnny!" I shouted again and again as I ran back toward our house hoping that I'd find him happily playing with General in our front yard. But there was no sign of anyone. I stood on the curb and shouted Johnny's name at the top of my lungs.

I kept shouting even as a steady stream of cars drove slowly by our house. Many of the drivers stared at me as though I were crazy. My throat burned from yelling and I started to sit on the curb to think about my next move when a yellow Buick convertible pulled up. A middle-aged man wearing a Cowboys cap jumped out of the driver's seat and ran over to me. "Say," he said, "are you looking for your son, by any chance?"

"Oh, yes, I'm looking for Johnny," I said. The man described a little boy wearing red pajamas being led by a German shepherd.

"They were about four blocks away just five minutes ago," said the man. "I tried to talk to the little boy. I could see there was something wrong with him, but that dog wouldn't let me get anywhere near him."

Without further words exchanged, I ran around to the passenger side of the car, jumped in, and the man drove — fast — to where he had last seen Johnny. We came to a busy intersection with a fast-food restaurant on one corner and a gas station across the street. My head started to pound and I impatiently rubbed my thighs as I watched the traffic speed by us. We sat in the car, stopped at the traffic light. I looked to my right and there was General, a few hundred yards away, walking slowly across the street, and Johnny was holding on to his collar, plodding alongside him, the feet of his red pajamas, blackened with dirt, were now torn, exposing his toes. The traffic came to a halt as people screeched on their brakes and rolled down their windows to stare at these two incongruous figures. General was patiently guiding Johnny around the cars and over to the other side of the street. I hopped out of the Buick, ran between the cars, and scooped Johnny up in my arms, kissing him and smoothing his hair. He seemed completely unfazed by his adventure and gave me one of his adoring smiles. General looked up at me with his big brown sorrowful eyes and I put Johnny down and gave General a big hug.

Because of a Dallas city ordinance we were required to keep

General fenced in the backyard when we were gone during the daytime. In College Station he had been used to roaming the neighborhoods, and when we first arrived in Dallas we thought we'd have to give him away. But now there was no way we were ever going to let go of our cherished dog.

That day I decided that I wanted Johnny at Saturday practices with me; I wanted him by my side. But I wasn't quite sure about how he'd be received. He had gone with me to practice while I was at A&M, but that was at the end of my time there. I really wanted him to be accepted by the Cowboys players, but I wasn't sure how they would respond to him. I thought to myself those first few weeks, Here's an assistant coach moving into Dallas with five children and one of them has Down syndrome! Do the coaches and players accept that? Would all these big-name players — guys like Roger Staubach, Lee Roy Jordan, and Mel Renfro, household names to many people across the country — take Johnny in? What about Tom Landry, one of the top coaches in the NFL — a disciplined, tough coach, how would he feel about having Johnny walking around the locker room and talking to the players? I didn't necessarily think that they would be cruel, but I worried that they might ignore him. I had the same uncertain feelings and questions about whether we would be accepted all over again, just as I had when we moved from Tuscaloosa to College Station.

I still didn't know the people on the staff well. Bobby Franklin, my predecessor as secondary coach, who had been moved over to coaching special teams, was popular with the other Cowboy coaches and players. Some people on the staff acted a little cool toward me, and I knew that they didn't particularly like the fact that I'd never been to a pro camp or played pro ball like Bobby, and that I hadn't really enjoyed great success at Texas A&M either.

I was struggling trying to learn a whole new system, a new terminology, and a new way of handling the players. I always thought that a college player respected his coach just because he was his coach. But I was finding out that a professional player had a tendency to respect a guy who had played professional football first. You had to earn the respect of the pro. If a player was beaten for a long pass or he got a defensive misread, it was up to me to tell him what happened when he came off the field. A veteran player's not going to stand for the coach who didn't see the play or can't explain why he failed.

Finally, after we had won a few games, I felt that it might be a good time to ask Tom Landry if I could bring Johnny to practice with me. Tom was receptive to the idea. So, on the following Saturday morning in the fall of 1972, I asked Johnny while we were having breakfast if he'd like to come along with me.

"Sure, Pop!" he said and gave me a hug.

As we drove over to the field, I explained to Johnny how important it was for him to be polite to everybody he met. Even though I knew that he'd have no trouble being mannerly when he greeted the players and Coach Landry, I kind of enjoyed giving him some fatherly advice on shaking hands and looking at people straight in the eye when he first met them, and I told him some of the players' names.

We walked into the locker room, where a lot of the players were changing their clothes, and I introduced Johnny to a few of the guys. He was charming, and I stood by, watching as he looked up at some of these huge players who were three times his size, made eye contact with them, and shook hands. I spotted Coach Landry in the corner and I took Johnny over to visit with him. "Johnny, I'd like for you to meet Coach Landry," I said.

"Hi, Tom. " Johnny smiled and gave him a firm handshake.

As Johnny and I left the locker room and walked onto the field I bent down and whispered to him, "Son, you've got to call the coach 'Coach Landry.' Do you think that you can do that?"

127

"Yes sir," said Johnny.

The next week as I was driving to practice I gently reminded him of our conversation about greeting Coach Landry.

And that next week Johnny walked right up to him, shook his hand, and said, "Hi, Tom." It happened every time. Coach Landry didn't seem to mind at all because 95 percent of his players called him Tom. That's the way it was in the pros. I knew that Coach Landry liked Johnny, and I could see that despite his reputation as an unfeeling and businesslike man he was really very caring. But coming out of college football, it just didn't sound right to me when Johnny called him by his first name. In fact, I never could bring myself to call him Tom. To me, he was always Coach Landry.

Saturday practice during the season usually began around 9 A.M., and since it was on the eve of the next game it was always sort of low-key. The rookies would bring in all kinds of doughnuts, cream filled, glazed, sugarcoated, and they'd set them out on a tray. From the first day that Johnny came with me I noticed that one of the players always made sure Johnny could pick out the doughnut that he wanted. It was no big deal to anybody but me, but whether it was the equipment people, some of the players, or the children of the players, I was always aware of who included Johnny and who didn't. It was like I was wearing radar. I noticed anyone who was the least bit kind to him and I remembered that person for a long time.

Many of the players started bringing their children, and I enjoyed watching them as they included Johnny when they ran around the field, played a game of catch, or stood by the sidelines and watched the practice. They genuinely seemed to like Johnny, and for the first time ever I watched children, other than my girls, respond positively to his sunny disposition and gentle nature. When we'd drive home together he'd talk to me about the various children he had met, and he was asking to see them again. For the first time ever, Johnny was making friends with children other than the ones he met at school.

Very few Saturdays would go by that one of the players wouldn't give him a ball. Then, by the end of the practice, he would usually end up giving it to one of the players' children before he went home. The players were always surprised and touched by his generosity, but for years I'd seen how he was always thinking about others and wanting to make them happy.

He liked to stand at the sidelines with me as I coached, and I'd try and go over plays with him and describe a little about what was happening. He was attentive as I told him about the players, their positions, and what they were supposed to do, and there were many times when I'd forget a player's name for an instant and I'd turn to Johnny. Every time I asked him, he'd give me the right answer. I was beginning to see that he had an incredible gift: once he met someone he never forgot a face.

A couple of months after Johnny had started to go to practices, the head trainer, Don Cochran, came up to me and asked if I thought Johnny would like to help tape up players' ankles and ice their swollen feet. A few minutes later I watched Johnny follow him off to the locker room. They didn't come back, and a few hours later, after practice was over, I went to look for them. There was Johnny talking with the players, methodically rolling tape around one of the players' ankles while Don helped him. He didn't even notice when I came into the locker room.

Now when we'd head over to practice on Saturday mornings Johnny was often the first one to get into the car. We couldn't be late because he had an official job with Don Cochran as a trainer. He was starting to get to know the players better, and I could tell that they were enjoying getting to know Johnny.

One Saturday afternoon I saw Johnny sitting on the bench in the locker room holding court with Roger Staubach, our quarterback, and Lee Roy Jordan, our middle linebacker, who had had an All-American career at Alabama under Coach Bryant, and I overheard Johnny and him talking about Coach Bryant. Lee Roy was repeating one of Coach's favorite words of advice: "And then Coach Bryant said to us, 'If you're ahead, play like you're behind, and if you're behind, play like you're ahead.' " Johnny had heard me repeat the same story and he loved hearing it again, and then I heard him telling something about Coach Bryant. I tried listening to what Johnny was saying; maybe it was the story of our Junction trip, or it could have been the Cotton Bowl story. It didn't really matter, it seemed like Roger and Lee Roy were understanding exactly what Johnny was saying and wanting more stories. Johnny was loving their attention, and I saw that as long as the players would sit there, Johnny would just keep right on talking with them.

On another Saturday I stood over at the corner of the locker room and watched Johnny make believe that he was a kicker. He had seen one of the guys acting as the referee and pretending they were starting a game. Johnny took the ball from the guy and squeezed it, then when the "referee" blew his imaginary whistle, Johnny acted like he was kicking the ball. He started to laugh and the players laughed along with him, and I knew that he was providing them with a relief from the pressures of football, and at the same time the players were providing friendship and fun for Johnny. They liked performing this little routine, and I noticed that every time Johnny took the ball from the "referee" he'd always squeeze it first. I wondered why he did this and so one day I decided to ask the kicker. He explained that most kickers squeezed the ball right when they got it to check out the air pressure and see how far the ball might actually go. Now when I watched games I saw the kickers do this every time, and I realized that Johnny had seen it when he watched football on television.

Sometimes he would act like the quarterback and call out the signals. The players loved to tease him and Johnny quickly learned to tease them back. And always, after he had visited with them and it was time for us to go, he'd stand up and give them each a hug. I watched as these great big men, some of them two feet taller than Johnny and well over two hundred pounds, hugged him back.

By the end of the 1972 regular season we had a 10–4 record and the Cowboys had qualified for the playoffs — for the seventh year in a row, which was some kind of record. I was excited and tense as we approached the first-round playoff game. Roger Staubach passed for two touchdowns in the last minute and a half, which gave us a thrilling 30–28 victory over San Francisco, but a week later we had a disappointing loss to Washington. Johnny was gradually becoming empathetic when we lost games and I often found myself turning to him for comfort and solace. He'd come into my bedroom at night and give me an extra big hug, sit with me there for a while and hold my hand, and it made me feel a whole lot better.

Johnny had started to come to our home games, and he and Ruth Ann would sit in the back of the press box and she'd tell me how members of the press and fans would come up to them throughout the game and call Johnny by name. After the games, Don Cochran always asked him if he'd like to help out with the players in the locker room. One Sunday after we had beaten St. Louis, Lee Roy Jordan approached me and said, "You know, Gene, I think that Johnny has brought out a humanness in some of us that we were never able to express." He said that he had never really known anyone like Johnny before.

Cliff Harris and Charlie Waters were constantly being asked to lend their names for charity events, and they told me that they often had to say no because of time pressures. "Just knowing Johnny as well as we do makes me realize how important it is to go the extra mile and reach out to people," Cliff said. He told me that there were times when he was playing and practicing that he felt so focused and he was concentrating so intensely that he lost touch with reality, and Johnny helped him bring everything back into perspective. Other players told me that there were times when they had taken their athletic abilities for granted, until they met Johnny.

It wasn't just the players and their children who were responding so positively to him. Many nights when I'd come home from work I'd find that his teacher, Nancy Hall, had stopped by the house after school. She'd help him with his homework and bring him some kind of a treat — a notebook with designs on it, a chocolate bar, or a fancy pen or pencil set. She lived close by and whenever we would drive past her house, Johnny would make up a song with her name in it and sing it in the car. He talked about Nancy constantly and we could see that they had a special bond. He brought home flash cards almost every night and the girls started quizzing him until he learned about twenty-five or thirty words. He learned the alphabet and he and the girls would walk around the house singing the alphabet song at the top of their lungs. He also started to learn numbers. And now, when the girls brought their friends home from school, the first thing they'd do would be to take them to meet Johnny and then proudly show how many words he could identify off the flash cards. They wanted him to learn and they knew he was capable. He became so confident that he even tried to do some of Jackie's school assignments.

Finally, he entered the stage where he was no longer getting into dangerous objects. We could leave him in the kitchen for a while without worrying that he'd open the knife drawer, break glasses and plates, or suddenly disappear. It was a lot more peaceful at home because now we had only Martha Kate to watch carefully.

As Jackie turned ten and Johnny approached twelve I could see that more and more they were becoming each other's confidantes. When he first arrived home from school, he would wait for her and together they would make themselves a snack of anything that was in the refrigerator and then disappear into the den and turn on the television. The two of them stayed there, sometimes nestled under a blanket that they had made into a tent, until dinnertime. Other days they'd get the moon wagon out and fly down the driveway. Jackie had little physical fear and she could count on Johnny to be her partner. Jackie had always been a sort of role model to Johnny, but now an even closer bond was forming. He didn't really have to tell her how he was feeling; she always seemed to know exactly what was going on in his mind. If Johnny was upset about something, Jackie would often come to us and tell us what was going on. It was years later that Jackie told us how Johnny would often confide in her about some of the children in the classroom that he didn't like, or he'd tell her who had misbehaved, or he'd talk about a child who was mean to him and he'd tell her what the teacher had done about it. I'm sure he was a little afraid to tell Ruth Ann and me about some of the negative things at school because he was aware how happy we were that he was attending classes.

In our minds Johnny's school proved to be everything we could ever have dreamed of and more. We noticed how much Johnny's speech had improved as a result of the speech therapy he had been getting. He had become more self-assured because he could talk and be understood, and more and more he was joking and teasing.

For the first time, Johnny was learning to cut paper, and now he could color a little and write his first name, something he was extremely proud of. He'd have me sit down at the kitchen table with him and he'd get a sheet of paper and a pencil and slowly, in an awkward sort of way, he would painstakingly write one letter of his name at a time in cursive. When he was done he went over every letter to make sure that it looked perfect and then he'd hold it up for me to see. He started bringing home work sheets that the girls helped him with and he'd have other homework assignments where he'd have to sort and match different shapes and objects.

And for the very first time Johnny was invited to his classmates' birthday parties, and he started giving parties too. Johnny's best friends in the class were the other children who had Down syndrome. They seemed to seek each other out and gravitate toward one another.

In the late fall of 1975, we received a letter from Johnny's school declaring that his class was going to be mainstreamed in physical education in a few months. The school had decided to start doing this during the spring semester and the children would be playing softball. I had no idea what mainstreaming was or how it worked and I felt some anxiety as I read and reread the letter.

Whenever I heard that Johnny was going to try something for the first time, my initial reaction would be one of pure happiness and excitement. But then after a while I'd start getting nervous, and inevitably I'd end up worrying over whether he'd be accepted, or if he could physically handle the challenge, or if people would tease him. It bothered me that I was so overly protective, and I knew, of course, that if I was going to do the right thing by Johnny I'd have to let go a little more.

One evening there was a meeting at the school about the new law, PL94–142, which had been passed on November 29, 1975, and signed by President Gerald Ford. Ruth Ann and I were told that the new legislation was responsible for Johnny mainstreaming in physical education and we were curious to learn more about the laws affecting his schooling. The principal of the school stood up and introduced a panel of experts and then had the parents ask questions.

A panel member explained that the legislation guaranteed every child an appropriate education in the least restrictive environment possible, no matter what the child's disability. "It's only the beginning and it's very exciting," said a mother. "You know that physical education is one of the easiest subjects for children to be mainstreamed in, because teachers don't have to make many changes in the classrooms. Everyone benefits because the 'normal' children will have the opportunity to be with children with disabilities. If it works I'm sure that they'll eventually be able to be mainstreamed in subjects like reading and math."

"I'm completely against mainstreaming and I don't care what subject it's in," said another parent. "I don't want the other children to be mean to my son."

Many of them thought this might well be the very beginning of full inclusion for their children and I could see that the idea of sending their children to school all day alongside other children who weren't disabled was upsetting to some of them.

I found it comforting that a lot of the parents I spoke to after the meeting were as nervous as I was about the softball program. One father told me that he was worried that the able-bodied children would be mean to his daughter, who had cerebral palsy, and he was bothered that the very law intended to help his child might in reality backfire and hurt her by exposing her to other children who were not considerate. That night as we left the meeting, I asked Ruth Ann how she felt about Johnny playing softball. I thought that maybe in the back of her mind she was worried, too. But she didn't show it. I could see that she was so excited for Johnny that he was finally going to be able to play sports with a wide group of children, and she assured me that everything would work out fine.

We had started the 1975 season with nobody really expecting the Cowboys to be a championship contender. Over the last three seasons we had lost twice in the playoffs and failed to qualify the third year, and it seemed to me that everyone thought we were leveling off. But Coach Landry seemed more geared up than ever to prove sportswriters and fans wrong. At the end of the season, after just beating the Jets, we were facing Minnesota in the first round of the playoffs and Coach Landry had indeed proved them wrong.

There was a great deal of tension because if we beat them we'd automatically be in the championship game, which might then lead to the Super Bowl. I was putting in long hours at work and I was tense and exhausted. We all needed a little rest, but I knew it was more important for us to get the team ready to play than to rest.

That year on Christmas Eve, as our family was gathered around the piano singing carols, we heard a tapping on the window and there was Santa Claus waving and shouting out, "Merry Christmas to the Stallings family!" We were all so excited that we ran out the front door to see him and he started running down the street as we all followed behind, trying to catch him. Christmas was always such fun in our house, and one of the reasons was that Johnny believed in Santa, and does to this day. Johnny tried to keep up with all of us, but I saw that he was winded and I stopped with him when we were halfway down the street, just where Santa's hat fell off, and hung back with him. Pretty soon Santa (who was in reality our neighbor from across the street) came back, and as Johnny hugged him we invited him back into the house to get warm and sing with us. Johnny kept feeling his soft white beard and patting his huge stomach as we all sang. That night we left our traditional grapefruit half out for Santa, and Johnny told me as I tucked him in that he was sure that Santa would help the Cowboys go to the Super Bowl.

On December 28 we beat Minnesota and once again Roger Staubach played superbly. With less than two minutes left we were losing 14–10, but Staubach completed five passes, the last one a 50-yarder to Drew Pearson for the winning touchdown. Right after New Year's we beat Los Angeles, and Staubach threw four touchdown passes. Now we were headed for the Super Bowl to play against Pittsburgh. I always thought that a national championship game was big, but this was the ultimate. The game was to be in Miami's Orange Bowl that year. I wasn't prepared for the huge traffic jams and long lines in restaurants that we encountered a few days before the game. Media from all over the world were there and all of our players and coaches were constantly being interviewed the week before the big day.

At halftime, I thought we would win, but then Pittsburgh came on strong, intercepting a few passes in the second half, and they won a very competitive Super Bowl X, with the final score 21–17. That night Willie Nelson's band performed nearby, but few of the players ventured out to hear the music. We were all greatly disappointed with the loss. But I tried to tell the players that we had been a wild card team and hadn't been given much of a chance to make it to the Super Bowl with our 8–6 regular season record. Still, spirits were low and there was complete silence on the team plane the next day as we flew back to Dallas.

A couple of months later, we received a note from Johnny's teacher that softball would be starting soon and that Johnny had been chosen to be the pitcher of his team. All of the fears that I had about him playing softball suddenly vanished and I felt proud and excited. I went out and bought new bats, gloves, and bases the next day after work, and now when I'd get home the children and I would practice softball in the backyard and Johnny would always be the pitcher. Over the years the girls had played all kinds of ball out in the backyard with Johnny, but I didn't pay much attention and I was surprised to find that he had a lot of natural ability.

Right away I could see that he was going to be a solid pitcher. He had a good strong arm, took his time, and was consistent, and I found myself bragging about his new position on the team to anybody who would listen. There wasn't a night that went by when one of the girls wouldn't ask about how he was doing on the softball team. He loved the game, there was no doubt about it, but what he talked about most were his new friends.

One warm spring afternoon I decided I just had to leave work an hour early and go out and watch them play. I drove out to his school, making sure that I parked my car in the lot farthest away from the playing field so that Johnny and his teachers wouldn't see me. Then I walked out to the side of the field and stood next to a big maple tree. I felt a little foolish as I ducked behind the tree every time Johnny or one of his teachers seemed to look over my way. Johnny stood a few feet off the pitching mound, outfitted in a bright blue vest, and I could see that he was really concentrating as he slowly wound up and then pitched a perfect ball to a cute little redheaded girl who had Down syndrome.

"Strike one!" the teacher yelled. The outfielders, dressed in the same vests as Johnny, shouted, "Strike her out, Johnny! You can do it! Strike her out!" Johnny paused, looked back at his team members, and smiled.

I surveyed the field. The little boy playing first base looked like maybe he had cerebral palsy. He dragged his left leg as he walked and his hands looked tight — he kept banging his gloved hand together with his bare hand. The second and third basemen appeared to be nondisabled girls, as was the right fielder. The shortstop was a little boy with Down syndrome.

Johnny wound up and pitched again. The redheaded little girl belted the ball. I shaded my eyes with my hand and whistled to myself as I watched the ball fly up in the air, right above Johnny's head. Then I held my breath and watched as he paused, looked up into the sky, and then almost as an afterthought stuck out his mitt at just the right angle and caught the ball. There was loud cheering from the outfielders as they ran in and patted Johnny on the back. Some of the boys from the regular, or nondisabled, classroom towered over Johnny, and I was surprised that eighth graders could be so beefy and tall. I looked over at Johnny as the children continued to surround him and cheer, and I had to stop myself from clapping and yelling too.

When it was his turn up at bat, he swung hard at the first two balls that were pitched to him. But when the next pitch came at him, he connected, whacking it good and hard. He stopped, watched as the ball bumped along the field past the shortstop, and then he gently placed the bat down on the ground. I watched as he shuffled off to first base and I thought how the doctor said he no longer needed to take digitalis, his heart medicine. We never tried to stop him now from doing anything physical. But as the outfielder scrambled to throw the ball to first I noticed that Johnny's face was very pale. His skin was the color of pearls and I could see as he landed on base how breathless he was.

"Safe!" called the teacher-umpire as Johnny stood solidly on the base. The next batter was an able-bodied little girl who hit a long fly ball way past the right fielder. Johnny got mixed up and started to run toward third base, but one of the children dashed out to the field and led him to second, then to third, then home as the batter followed patiently behind Johnny. His team won 3–0, and his teammates jumped up and down, picked each other up, yelled, and carried on. I walked back to my car thinking how well coordinated Johnny was, and for an instant I thought that maybe, just maybe, he would have been a good football player. Once again I had a vision of a strapping son running down the field cradling a football as I stood by on the sidelines watching. That night at the dinner table he talked about the game and how his team had won and then he went on and on about all of his friends. As I sat there and listened to his happy chatter that night, I doubt you could have found a prouder father in Dallas.

CHAPTER 7

SCHOOL DAYS

A FEW days later, Jackie asked Johnny about his softball team at the dinner table. "That part of physical education is over now," Ruth Ann said abruptly and went back to eating. There was a momentary silence and then the girls started talking about something else. I tried to read the expression on Ruth Ann's face, but I couldn't tell what she was thinking. I didn't dare ask her about it then because I really didn't want to know the truth.

That night I read until almost 2 A.M. Finally, when I started to get sleepy and I was putting my book down and turning off the lights, I heard a strange low sound, almost like a moaning. I listened carefully as it got louder, then softer and then louder again. I jumped out of bed and walked out into the hallway and stood quietly, listening. But the sound had stopped and I started to go back to bed, thinking maybe I had been dreaming. But as I walked back to my room, I heard the moaning louder than before. It was definitely coming from Johnny's room and I raced down the hall and opened his door. There he was sitting on his chair in the pitch-

140

dark room in his red pajamas and he was singing hymns. I flicked on the light and saw that he was also performing the hanger trick: two metal hangers were positioned on his middle and index finger and he had the hangers going back and forth.

"Hi, Pop!" Johnny looked up when the light went on, and kept right on swinging the hangers.

"Son, it's very late," I said, taking the hangers from him and putting them down in the corner of his room. "You've got to go to bed and get some sleep." I tucked him in, gave him a kiss, and turned out the light.

The next night I woke with a start. "Bebes!" Ruth Ann grabbed my arm. "What is that strange sound?" I led her down the hallway and opened Johnny's door, flicked on his light, and there he was as though he had never left the chair from the night before, singing hymns, completely unaware of anyone around him, and he had the hangers swinging fast — back and forth.

"John Mark, this has got to stop. You are going to be completely worn out tomorrow unless you get in bed right away," I said as I took the hangers from him and hid them in the back of his closet. Johnny didn't seem too upset by my stern tone of voice as he climbed into bed.

Ruth Ann and I stayed awake for hours wondering if Johnny was trying to comfort himself in some way. Again, I thought about his softball being canceled and I wondered if that was on his mind and if he missed playing, but I didn't bring it up.

For the next few months Johnny continued staying up late at night, singing and performing his trick. I eventually stopped going into his room and now I'd hear the low singing almost every night. But during the day he seemed perfectly fine — eager to go to school, cheerful and rested, and I thought that maybe the singing brought him some kind of contentment and calm.

At the end of May, we attended an informal graduation ceremony for Johnny and all of the other fourteen-year-olds in his special education class. The other eighth graders, who would be leaving Lake Highlands Elementary for the high school down the street, were having their ceremony in a separate part of the school. The children in special education would be attending the Cooperative Training Center (CTC), a facility housed in a converted Safeway grocery store, for children with special needs only, which was about two miles from our house.

As Ruth Ann, Johnny, and I were leaving the ceremony, I felt a tap on my back. I turned around and saw a young father standing with his arm around the shoulder of a big, blond boy who looked to be in the regular eighth-grade class.

"Hi, I'm Joe, and this is my son, Steve."

I shook his hand, introduced myself, and then introduced Johnny and Ruth Ann.

"I just wanted to tell you that Stevie here, well, he really enjoyed being on the softball team with your son," the father said.

Johnny smiled and gave Steve a high five. "Thanks for letting us know that," I said. The father and son started to walk away but I called out to Joe. "Would you mind if I called you later tonight?"

"Not at all." He took a pen out of his pocket and jotted his home phone number down on the back of his business card and handed it to me.

After the children had gone to bed, I called Joe and asked him why the school had so suddenly stopped the softball program. There was a long silence on the other end and then he told me that there had been a great deal of pressure from the parents of "able-bodied children" to discontinue mainstreaming. Joe said that many parents had complained to school officials. "I was one of the few parents who thought it was a good idea. You know, Steve learned so much from your son this past spring."

I thanked Joe and quickly hung up the phone. I couldn't believe what he had just told me and I went into the other room to find Ruth Ann and tell her about my conversation. But it turned out that she had known about the parents complaining all along and she couldn't bring herself to tell me. After my initial shock wore off, I started to get angry and I asked Ruth Ann whom I should speak to at the school. She and I talked late into the night, finally deciding not to say anything at all. In some strange way I felt sorry for the parents who complained, and although deep down I could understand their concerns, it didn't make me feel any better.

I'm sure the reason we didn't speak up to the principal of the school or to the president of the PTA was because we had been so happy that Johnny had such a good public school close by in the neighborhood where he could go every day. After years of seeing little or no educational progress we were appreciative of such a good school system and didn't want to rock the boat.

That June I looked forward to our month at the farm more than ever. Mr. Henry greeted us with a long list of chores that needed to be done and he and I set out to work, rising at five-thirty every morning and working side by side until lunchtime. After a while I found myself talking about Johnny. Mr. Henry was a good listener, and I surprised myself at how upset I sounded relaying all the details of his softball team, how the games had suddenly been canceled, and my conversation with Joe.

The afternoons I would spend time with the children, riding horseback together, taking long hikes through the meadow, and riding on the tractor with Johnny. I could see that his appearance was changing. He had been such a cute-looking little boy and now, at fourteen, his teeth seemed way too big for his mouth and his slanted eyes were more pronounced than they had ever been. He was starting to get acne all over his pale little face and he was still much shorter than other children. He was still a bit fragile and by the afternoon he was tired and listless. I'd find him napping on many afternoons and I wasn't sure if he didn't feel well or if it was because he was staying up so late at night. But he never complained that he was tired, and if there was something we wanted him to do he'd always be up for doing it. His small stature (he was now about five feet tall), which had made him seem adorable, almost elflike, when he was younger, wasn't cute any longer and now he looked like a puny, gawky teenager. His blond hair had cowlicks in it, just like mine, and no matter what kind of goo we'd put on it or how we'd comb it, his hair just wouldn't stay down flat. But he still had the gorgeous blue eyes he'd always had.

In the fall of 1976 when Johnny started at his new school, CTC, people began to respond to him in a new way. In parks and shopping centers, even at the girls' schools, when Ruth Ann would have Johnny with her, people would often move away from them as though he were some kind of scary creature. This was a new phase, something we hadn't had to contend with during Johnny's early years. I found that when I was alone with Johnny, this kind of negative reaction from people didn't occur much, and I think it was because people recognized me as a Cowboy coach. They'd usually say something to me about a game or one of the players and then move on without responding to Johnny too much one way or another.

Now, when Ruth Ann went to PTA meetings, people whom she didn't know would sit down next to her and, seeing that Johnny was "retarded" and looked different, they would actually get up and move away. Ruth Ann would look over at Johnny and he'd have that sad little look on his face that we had seen too many times over the years when people slighted him. But our friends, who were more sensitive, would make a point of sitting down right next to them. They wanted to protect us and we loved them for that. Once again, I would think of Jack Horn, and now I wondered how he felt when we all screamed and ran away from him. Johnny

144

would always know when someone was rejecting him. Many times when he was in a situation and people were talking over his head or if they didn't try and understand him, he would shrug his shoulders and flip his hands up like he'd had enough.

As Johnny was turning the corner into adolescence, we were entering the stage that I had been anxious about ever since he was first born — the girls were dating and boys were coming over to the house more and more. I had no idea and no one to tell me what he would eventually look like as he was growing up, and I wondered if he would ever have seizures or become uncontrollable. I thought back to when Ruth Ann and I dated in high school and how self-conscious we and all the other teenagers were about people's appearances. I envisioned my girls being embarrassed about Johnny and perhaps isolating him when their dates came over.

Anna Lee was now in her senior year of high school, Laurie was a junior, Jackie was in fifth grade, and Martha Kate had just begun first grade. The older girls were on the drill team and involved with youth groups and church activities. The telephone rang all the time and it was usually for one of them. But now when the young men came over they knew Johnny from seeing him at football games, and I couldn't get over how kind most of them were with him. We never schooled Johnny on how to behave around the boys, and if he came into the room and was wearing something sort of inappropriate or he made funny sounds, the girls never acted embarrassed and they put the boys at ease. If any of their dates showed the slightest bit of discomfort with Johnny, the girls wanted nothing to do with them. They would measure whether they liked a guy by his acceptance of Johnny, and instead of being tense during this period, I was able to relax and take a great deal of pride in my children.

Around this time as May Allen, our baby-sitter, saw that Johnny was beginning to be accepted by the public and by the girls' friends and their boyfriends, she started talking to us about her own son, Greg, who we discovered had autism. Jackie was in the same class with Greg's brother, Timmy, and she'd come home and tell us stories about Greg, but in the four years that May worked for us she had never mentioned him.

One afternoon she approached Ruth Ann and asked what kinds of things Johnny was learning in school. That led to a further discussion about Greg, and Ruth Ann asked her if she'd like to bring him with her when she came to baby-sit. He was a handsome, sweet-looking boy, but he didn't speak.

When May first brought Greg over, he would go off into the corner by himself and spin a top over and over again and sit there for an hour mesmerized by the spinning. Or sometimes Greg would disappear and we'd find him hiding under the bed or in a corner. It was only when Johnny performed his hanger trick that Greg would reappear and sit and watch Johnny intently. Eventually May got Greg into Johnny's school and he began to be less isolated. I could see that she was beginning to dress Greg in more colorful clothes, and now when he came over he'd play a little more with Johnny, and May seemed almost proud of him.

Johnny took a bus the two miles to school that was provided free as a result of the 1975 legislation. The bus was supposed to pick him up and drop him off right in front of our house, but the driver could never get it quite right and he always pulled up across the street instead. Ruth Ann and I called the bus company to ask if the driver would make a U-turn on Ferndale and pick Johnny up in front of the house. Some drivers would do this, but others would not. We'd have to walk Johnny across the street and make sure that he got on the bus safely, and in the afternoon Ruth Ann or May would have to go across the street to pick him up.

The new laws forced schools to accommodate all children with disabilities who qualified for special education services. Suddenly, due to "Child Find," a federal mandate stating that all children from three to twenty-one had to be identified so that they could attend school, there was a great increase in the number of children who were entering school for the first time. It was each school system's responsibility to spread the word about the laws, and many schools put notices in newspapers and made announcements on the radio. Children with disabilities of all ages who had never attended school before were suddenly in the classroom, and the schools were not prepared. Some classes were now located in basements, storage rooms, or wherever space could be found.

Services such as social work assistance, speech pathology, and physical therapy were now centralized in one location at Johnny's new school and the students were bused in from all over the district. Just like at Lake Highlands Elementary, class size was large, but the lead teacher, Mary Hill, and part-time helpers and aides seemed to manage the children well. From the first day of school Mary showed a profound interest in Johnny. He was always the teacher's helper, and she knew she could count on him to take the lunch money to the office, to pass out school supplies, and to be a messenger between classrooms because he was so responsible and because of his superb social skills. From the first few days of school, she had the children creating wonderful art projects — airplanes, trucks, and cars out of papier mâché, large murals in bold colors that took up all the walls in the classroom, and she even had them make puppets out of felt and put on puppet shows. I don't know how she did it because we were also beginning to find out that she was struggling a good part of the day with some of the children who had severe behavioral problems and didn't belong in the same classroom with the other students. Occasionally Johnny would come home with stories of how a big girl named Louise had cussed at him or how she had screamed and yelled and disrupted the other children in the classroom.

Mary was always coming up with ideas for field trips. I'm not sure how she and only an assistant managed to take the class on various outings to the zoo and to museums, but they were always on the go. In the late spring she organized a camping trip to Lake Lavon, twenty minutes from Dallas, and since it was the off-season, I had the time to go with them.

The Friday night before we were to leave, Johnny and I went out to the garage and dug through all the old camping gear that I had bought when I was at A&M and hadn't used since then. We came up with two sleeping bags, a few flashlights, some rusty pots and pans, and a two-person tent. We brought the equipment out onto the living room floor and packed our clothes inside the sleeping bags. Then I told Johnny to sit on top of one of the sleeping bags because I had a present for him. "Close your eyes," I said. I went into the front hall closet and pulled out two brand-new fishing rods, a tackle box, and lures that I had bought especially for the trip. I walked back into the living room and Johnny was sitting on top of the sleeping bag with his hands pressed against his eyes.

"Okay, you can open your eyes now," I said.

Johnny uncovered his eyes and I handed him the rods and the tackle box. But he wasn't as excited as I had hoped. In fact, I think he was a little confused. I had always gone fishing every year for a few days with friends, but I had always thought Johnny wasn't quite ready to put the bait on the hook and sit quietly holding a fishing rod. I realized that I had never taken him fishing. I went over to the bookshelf and pulled an old photo album down and took out some pictures of me fishing when I was a boy of about Johnny's age. I felt as though I had been born with a fishing rod in my hands. I opened the photo album and saw a picture of myself sitting on my daddy's lap holding a fishing rod. I couldn't have been more than two and a half or three. There was one of Dad and me sitting on a rock, and then one of my brother, Jimmy, and me standing in sopping wet clothes, holding on to a large crappie at Lake Crook. Looking at those pictures brought back some happy memories. I had gotten a big fish on my line and called for Jimmy to help me reel it in and we both ended up falling in the lake. I smiled to myself and said to Johnny as I pointed to a picture of Dad and me sitting on a rock, fishing contentedly, "This is what you and I can do together at Lake Lavon tomorrow, son."

The next day Johnny and I packed the car with the camping equipment and we headed off on our trip. Lake Lavon had never looked prettier. The water was a turquoise blue and the trees had those light green buds on them that always makes me feel sort of excited, like summer's just around the corner. Many of the families had arrived and were unpacking their cars and setting up tents. Johnny led me around the campground, taking his time to introduce me to the different children in his class. I could see that he had made close friends with most of them, and they'd hug one another and give each other pats on the back.

Mary came over to us and showed us where to pitch our tent. It was getting dark as we finished setting up camp, and Mary and some of the parents had made a big fire right near the lake. There were several pots boiling away and Johnny and I walked over to see what was going on and if we could help. Mary showed Johnny how to stir one of the pots and I watched him, a little nervous that he might get too close to the fire as he methodically stirred the pot. One of the fathers started playing the guitar and soon the children were gathered around him singing. The minute Johnny heard the music he stopped stirring and sat down with the others. I could hear his voice above all the others as he sang out, "This land is your land, this land is my land."

I looked up into the sky at the sliver of a moon, spotting the Big Dipper, and then the Little Dipper. I remembered how my father had taught me to draw a line from two stars in the Big Dipper to the North Star. The smells of baked beans and chicken cooking over an open fire filled the brisk air and I walked back over to our tent to get sweaters for Johnny and me.

As I was unzipping the tent a high-pitched screaming cut through the still night, and I whirled around and there at the campfire was Louise, screaming, kicking, and biting. Her mother was trying to calm her down, but Louise kicked more violently than ever and started spitting and cussing. I saw Mary make a dash for her tent and she came back carrying what looked like a large piece of canvas. Louise was screaming and crying and trying to get loose from her mother, who had her held down on the ground. Mary calmly unrolled the piece of canvas and called out to me and a few other of the parents to bring Louise over to her.

I realized then that she was going to put Louise in a straitjacket. I had only read stories about this kind of thing, had never actually seen it, and the idea scared me. I looked over at Johnny as two other fathers, Louise's mother, and I carried Louise over to Mary.

"Mary, isn't there some other way to calm her down?" I asked.

"No, she needs to be in the jacket for a while so she won't hurt herself, or others," she said. She rolled Louise up in the canvas squares and tied the belts around Louise's arms and legs. Mary was very gentle with Louise, who had not calmed down at all.

"It's going to be okay, baby," she said as she smoothed Louise's hair.

Louise was trussed up like a turkey, her arms tied securely to her sides and her legs sticking straight out in front of her. While Mary sweetly talked to her a little more, Louise stopped her carrying on. Johnny and the other children sat huddled by the fire and I went over to them and put my arm around Johnny. The father started playing the guitar again but none of the children were singing. Johnny started to cry a little and so did some of the others.

Mary disappeared with Louise into her tent while the parents and I quickly got dinner together and served it up to the children. We all sat and ate together quietly. A mother tried explaining what had happened with Louise. She told the children that Louise had different troubles from theirs, but they didn't really respond, and we all ended up going to bed early. No one really knew what set **Louise off, but now I remembered Johnny** complaining about her outbursts in school. It was obvious that she needed more supervision than the school was able to give. But at the time, all children with special needs were lumped together.

The next morning Johnny and I woke up as the sun was coming up over the hills. There was bacon frying on the fire and when I got out of the tent I saw that Mary and Louise were making breakfast with some of the other students. It was a calm, beautiful morning and when we greeted Mary and Louise I felt as if the outburst from the night before had never happened. Louise smiled and Mary talked about taking the children on a hike. But I wanted to go fishing alone with Johnny.

After breakfast, he and I walked about a quarter of a mile around the lake together. Johnny stopped to throw a couple of stones into the lake. I shielded the sun from my eyes with my hands and watched as the stones skimmed the surface and then disappeared in the water. He still had a good arm.

We came to a private little spot and found a big flat boulder to sit on. Johnny wanted to put his hands in the water and he took his shoes and socks off and we walked to the edge of the water and he stuck his toes in. "Cold, Pop!" he squealed and then he stuck both of his feet in.

"Come on, Pop, let's go swimming!" He splashed me.

"Too cold, Johnny," I said. "Come on, let's try fishing."

Johnny liked casting and we practiced flinging the rod back and forth several times until he really got the hang of it. We sat quietly together fishing, but my mind kept wandering to the night before.

I wished Johnny and Jackie could attend the same school. I thought that if the two of them could go to and from school together and see each other in the halls, it would be good for both of them since they were so close. We sat quietly together for an hour, without a bite. Johnny started to grow impatient and kept practicing his casting, but I told him to keep his line in the water and maybe something good would happen. And a few minutes later it did. I saw a pull on his line.

"You've got a bite, Johnny!" I shouted, getting up to help him. But I could see he didn't need me. He knew just what to do and started reeling in his line, and pretty soon we saw that he had caught a small sunfish. Johnny was so excited that he started to drop his pole in the water and I grabbed it from him just as it was about to slide into the lake. Together we took the sunfish off the hook and dropped it in our bucket. Johnny was fascinated by the fish swimming around in our little bucket. We tried fishing a little more but neither of us caught anything. It didn't matter because just sitting quietly together was my prize. After a while, I put my arm around Johnny and we walked back to the campground, our bucket with the precious fish in my hand. Johnny told everybody about the fish and all the children came racing over to get a good look at it. Finally, we headed home.

That Monday was dreary and rainy and I woke up with a terrible chest cold. I had a lot to do at the office, so even though I felt awful I decided to go to work anyway. As the day wore on, I felt worse and worse and I decided to go home early. At two-thirty I arrived home and May was there in the kitchen. I said a quick hello and went and lay down on the sofa in the living room and fell sound asleep. Minutes later, I was awakened by May yelling, "Oh no!" I jumped off the sofa, went to the front door where May was standing, and I saw a commotion out on the street. A blue sedan was stopped, the small yellow school bus with its red lights flashing in front of it, and it looked like somebody was lying on the ground. Then I saw that it was Johnny!

I dashed outside and there was a young woman kneeling over him. As I got closer to the crowd I saw that Johnny was sitting up and patting her on the back. I pressed through the group of neighbors who had suddenly gathered around and went right over to Johnny. Someone had covered his lower body with a bright red raincoat. He had a pained expression on his face, looking at the woman who was crying, making sure to comfort her and saying, "It's okay, it's all right."

"Johnny, what happened?" I asked him, expecting the worst.

"My ankle, Pop." Johnny moaned. "My ankle!"

In the distance I heard sirens.

"I didn't mean to . . . he just ran out . . . I couldn't stop!" the woman cried. Slowly I took the raincoat off Johnny, afraid of what I might see. I was sure that his ankle was crushed. But when I pulled down his sock his ankle was just red and puffy. There was no blood, just a bump and some swelling. Johnny sat up and started rubbing his ankle, all the while crying, "I'm hurt, I'm hurt."

The sound of sirens was deafening. I looked up to see an ambulance stopping a few feet from where I was bending over Johnny. Two paramedics jumped out, toting a stretcher. I stood up and watched them. Flashbacks of Johnny's emergency surgery in College Station filled my head and I held up my hands as if to tell them to back off. "I don't think it's that serious," I told them. "I think Johnny just needs to come on home and rest." But the paramedics pulled a stretcher out of the ambulance anyway and walked over with it to Johnny.

I turned to the woman who was crying and lashed out at her. "Why weren't you more careful? You could see that this child has Down syndrome!" My anger shocked the neighbors and it even surprised me. All Johnny's life I had been acutely aware that he

153

might not live another day, but I couldn't face the thought of his being hit by a car or killed in some kind of mindless accident.

A neighbor took me aside, explaining that the woman had been driving slowly in the rain but she hadn't seen the flashing lights of the school bus. I could see that the pavement was wet and that the lady had skidded right into him. "I can't understand how she wouldn't have seen the flashing lights," I said to my neighbor as I looked over at the woman and saw that she was now weeping harder than ever. Johnny was still patting on her back, trying to comfort her.

I had worked myself up into a real state, and I went over to the ambulance as the paramedics started to put Johnny on a stretcher. Despite my protests they took him to the hospital and gave him an X ray. Nothing was broken and the swelling around his ankle went down in a week. From that day on the bus stopped on our side of the street. But Johnny still complains of his ankle hurting from time to time.

IN the fall of 1977 the Cowboys were on a roll, winning their first eight games, which was their best start ever. I was beginning to feel comfortable coaching professional ball and becoming increasingly more confident in my coaching abilities. We finished the season with a 12–2 record and were the champions of the Eastern Division. We were headed to Super Bowl XII, against Denver, in New Orleans. Everyone was thrilled, including Johnny, and I was impressed by how astutely he had followed the games during the season. He started becoming knowledgeable about other NFL teams and knew the different teams' mascots, helmets, and colors. He loved winning just as much as I did, and I was glad that he would be coming to the Super Bowl with the rest of my family. We were a five-point favorite to defeat Denver and we won even more convincingly, by a score of 27–10. A few months later the players were presented with Super Bowl rings. I was caught off guard when Tom Landry called Johnny's name to receive a ring. Johnny slowly made his way up to the front of the room, and when Tom gave Johnny the diamond-studded ring Johnny hugged him and then, looking poised and confident, said, "Thank you, Tom!" The audience of coaches and players laughed at Johnny's familiarity with Coach Landry. The ring fit perfectly on Johnny's clubbed ring finger, and during the next few weeks whenever I would catch Johnny during a quiet moment I'd see him rubbing his hand over the large ring and counting the diamonds. Whenever anyone came over to the house, the first thing Johnny did was show off his Super Bowl ring.

That spring Mammy took a turn for the worse. I thought back to how she had come to our home immediately after Johnny's accident and how she was always there when we needed her. Johnny had had a hard time walking after being hit by the car and couldn't go to school for a week. She had stayed home with him, rubbing his ankle, putting ice packs on it, as she sat and read with him. But she had tired very easily and took naps in the middle of the day. Most nights by eight o'clock she'd be in bed sound asleep. I could tell that Ruth Ann was becoming more and more concerned about her, and that June while we were all at the farm she went over to her house and visited her every day.

Now it was Mammy's turn to be cared for. She had been her same sweet self and still told her little jokes to us, only this time we noticed that her tremors had extended to the neck, jaw, and legs. It was hard watching as she started shuffling and slowly became more stooped. Ruth Ann took dinner to her most nights, and toward the end of our stay at the farm, she was having trouble getting dressed in the morning. Just before we were leaving to go back to Dallas, Mammy's next-door neighbor called and told us that Mammy had had a stroke.

155

We knew then that we would have to put Mammy in a nursing home. Ruth Ann couldn't stop crying as the ambulance came to get her and took her to the hospital, and after she had stayed there a few days she was transferred to a nursing home in Paris. It had been very hard for Ruth Ann to visit her mother in a nursing home, where she inhabited a tiny dimly lit room and had none of her familiar possessions around her. She was only there a few short months, and in July she died. Right after her funeral I had to go to training camp just like I did every summer at Thousand Oaks, about forty-five miles north of Los Angeles. It was hard for me to leave, and I worried about my family and how they were coping after Mammy's death — especially Johnny. He had been so attached to her and had loved her dearly. Even when she was sick, she always had time for him.

That fall when I returned to Dallas, Ruth Ann and I were concerned how Johnny would handle the adjustment to another new school. He was having a hard time over Mammy's death, and when I'd go into his room at night he'd be talking to her picture that sat in a silver frame on his dresser. He couldn't express in words to us or anyone how he felt without Mammy, and he became withdrawn and melancholy. He missed the special dishes and desserts that Mammy prepared just for him, and now nobody had the time to read to him for long hours as Mammy had. Instead it seemed that we were all looking forward to the day that he would learn more and be able to use his talents. But Mammy never put that kind of pressure on Johnny. She had always accepted and loved him just because he was her grandson and he needed her. Now when he came home from school he didn't talk much about his day. His new school, still called Cooperative Training Center, was housed in yet another converted Safeway store not too far from our home. The law mandated that he would stay there until he was twenty-one years old. Johnny quickly grew close to his teachers there, Mr. Wiggle and Mr. Lynch, but we noticed that everyone in the group did the same thing every day, even if some people had the ability to do more. They all methodically put items in bags, stuffed envelopes, and performed assembly-line-type jobs. His school had become a workshop, and we were disappointed. But we understood that they were really trying to train Johnny so that he could someday perform a job. Even though we were thrilled that he was able to go to school, that the law gave special education students the right to a "free appropriate education in the least restrictive environment," sometimes Johnny's didn't seem appropriate. His work training seemed to be based on his academic weaknesses rather than on his strengths — his strong social skills and memory. Academically, he was unchallenged, and he no longer had the chance to go to neighborhood schools with his sisters. But through the PTA his school planned many outside activities and parties for each holiday. Johnny loved to socialize, and he would become very upset and start to cry if he had to miss an activity or a party. More and more he wanted to be with his own friends.

We started off the 1978 season with a mediocre six wins and four losses, and I thought there would be no way we could ever go to the Super Bowl that year. But suddenly the tables turned and we won six more games and then won the divisional playoffs against Atlanta and went on to defeat Los Angeles for the NFC championship. For the second year in a row, we were headed to the Super Bowl and we were playing Pittsburgh in a rematch of Super Bowl X, the first in Super Bowl history. However, we lost 35–31 and this was the most upset I had seen Johnny. He had known the thrill of winning the year before and he had the ring to prove it, and he had been avidly following the NFL teams on television. Of course, I wasn't happy with the loss, but this time the tables were turned and I found myself trying to console Johnny all that winter.

In June, after we had been at the farm a few days, our family paid a visit to the Roden Funeral Home to see Ruth Ann's cousin Marcus Roden. Marcus had been very helpful to us around the time of Mammy's death. As we walked along Church Street in Paris, I looked up at the big old funeral home thinking how it had been Marcus's father's dream to convert this grand home into a funeral parlor back when he bought it in the 1930s. When I was growing up my friends and I were in awe of the ornate mansion, with its tiled clay roof, third-story balcony, and stained glass windows. Surely it was the most lavish home in Paris, with twenty-eight rooms and ten bathrooms!

Johnny, Ruth Ann, and I opened the heavy door and went in and sat down in Marcus's office. After we had visited for a while, I started telling him about what Johnny was doing at CTC. After Johnny left the room I described the repetitiveness of some of the jobs he was doing.

"I didn't realize you were a working man," Marcus said to Johnny when he returned. "You should come work for me sometime."

"You'd let me work for you?" asked Johnny. He put his hand on Marcus's shoulder.

"Sure," said Marcus.

On the way home in the car Johnny kept saying, "I'm going to work for Cousin Marcus in the funeral home."

"You can go and work for Marcus sometime, dear," said Ruth Ann.

"No, I'm going to work for Marcus now," said Johnny.

That fall, back in Dallas, I discovered that Johnny had told all the players that he was going to work for his cousin Marcus, and they started coming up asking me about Johnny's new job. There was hardly a night that went by when Johnny wouldn't mention the job in the funeral home to me.

Finally I had to call Marcus and ask him if he really meant what he said.

"If Johnny wants to work for me that bad, then let him do it," said Marcus. "The next time you're out at the farm, call me. If there's a funeral, Johnny can work." Marcus paused. "I think this would be good for him and me."

That season right after we had beaten Washington, we headed out to the farm for Christmas. As soon as we walked in the door, Johnny told me to call Marcus. There was a funeral scheduled for the next afternoon and Marcus said he was glad I had called because he could use Johnny's help. When I announced this to Johnny, he ran to his room and put on his favorite sports jacket and ran downstairs.

"Ready, Pop," Johnny announced.

"One more day, Johnny," I said.

The next day Johnny got all dressed up in his Sunday best, gray flannel slacks, a white shirt and rep tie, and his navy blue sports jacket. I drove him over to the funeral parlor, not exactly sure what Marcus had in mind for him to do. When we got there mourners were starting to arrive and Marcus came out to greet us.

"I thought we'd have Johnny open the door for the people who are coming into the funeral home," he said.

Johnny smiled and went with Marcus. I stood over to the side as people started pouring through the door. I noticed the empathetic expression on Johnny's face as some of them came in crying, and a couple of times I saw Johnny pat somebody on the back.

After the last person had gone in, Marcus came out, thanked Johnny, and praised him. Johnny made sure that Marcus knew he would be available the next time there was a service. The very next week there were two funerals and Marcus called and asked Johnny to work both times, opening the door. Soon Marcus was calling frequently for Johnny when we were at the farm in June, and he started adding to Johnny's duties. Sometimes he'd have him work the tape deck that provided music at the service, and other times he'd have him drive up to the cemetery with the preacher and open the car door for him. I'd drop Johnny off, do some errands around town, and then came back to get him. One day when I arrived to pick Johnny up, Marcus pulled me over to the side.

"We've had quite an eventful day," he said. "I needed Johnny to ride with the minister and me up to the cemetery today. I was driving, the minister was in the front passenger seat, and Johnny was right behind him in the backseat. As we pulled up to the cemetery, the preacher bent down to read his notes and Johnny patted him on the shoulder from behind and kept saying to him, 'That's okay, you're going to be all right.' Johnny thought the preacher was crying!"

We both laughed, but then Marcus turned serious when he told me about the calming effect that Johnny had on the mourners, how he was very mannerly and personable and didn't seem to be afraid of death. "I'd like to bring him on as part of my staff," said Marcus. "He's a very important part of the operation here."

Johnny started working at the Roden Funeral Home more frequently, and Marcus increased his duties from opening the door and operating the recording equipment to greeting people and helping to set up chairs and supplies for the services. One summer day Johnny wanted his sisters to join him. After Johnny had worked the funeral that his sisters attended at his request, he snuck them up the servants' stairway to the third floor, where the caskets were kept in what had once been the elegant twenty-eight-hundred square-foot ballroom. According to Jackie, Johnny was particularly fascinated by the baby caskets and he couldn't wait to show them off. It was pitch-dark and Jackie had brought along a flashlight. As they were poking around and climbing in and out of the caskets, a deep booming voice out of nowhere bellowed, "You can see a lot better with the lights on!" Paul Gene, Marcus's brother, laughed as he flipped on the lights and watched the children jump out of the caskets, scared out of their wits.

To some people, working in such an environment might seem strange, but Johnny liked working there and I could see his confidence growing. For the first time he was performing a job that was using his talents: his excellent social skills, his steadiness, and his reliability. He was working with the public and he loved it, and from what Marcus told us people seemed to gravitate toward him because he was so empathetic. I could tell from the way he talked to us at the supper table that he was energized by a job that involved interacting with others. He was finally being challenged.

I recalled how our family would sometimes go to Wyatt's Cafeteria, a Texas-based chain, for a late supper in Dallas, and one night while we were having a hamburger we noticed a friendly, pretty girl named Cheryl, who had Down syndrome, clearing the tables. Johnny was taken with her and we started going regularly because she and Johnny would talk together a lot. Then one night when we went there we noticed Cheryl wasn't there. It turns out that Wyatt's had fired her because she talked to so many people that she wasn't getting her work done. But her loyal customers protested and finally Wyatt's hired her back. After Johnny's experience at the funeral home I could see how important it was for Cheryl to be working with the public.

About the time Johnny started working at the funeral home, some big American companies began to hire people with mental and physical disabilities. One of the forerunners, and one of the most innovative programs, was the McDonald's McJobs program, which was started in 1981 and has been highly successful ever since. In fact, they have employed over nine thousand people with mental and physical disabilities, and many of these employees work with the public every day.

Several years ago, the lives of our friends Jim and Peg Harrison changed when they had a grandchild, John Michael, who was born with Down syndrome. Jim, the CEO and chairman of the Harco

Drug and Carport Automotive chain, which has 150 outlets located throughout the South, has always been committed to hiring people with disabilities, but he stepped up his commitment dramatically upon the birth of his grandson. The people Jim hires have all kinds of disabilities, such as spinal cord injuries, cerebral palsy, and Down's, and they perform a host of jobs like cleaning, sweeping, mopping, clerical work, and restocking shelves, according to their skills. For many of these employees, working at Harco is the first time they have earned their own money.

Johnny also began getting involved with the Special Olympics around the time he started working at the funeral home. I had always thought the Special Olympics was nothing more than a few little games for children who had disabilities. But a friend from church had a daughter who was involved, and she strongly urged us to go and watch. Ruth and I went to the stadium and heard the young people with disabilities recite a Special Olympics pledge saying that they would try and do their best and be brave in the attempt. Johnny was with us that day and I could tell that he was fascinated with the athletes who marched around the stadium carrying colorful banners and by the many talented participants who ran fast and were members of bowling, volleyball, and basketball teams. He wanted to be a part of the action, and the next year he started running twenty- and forty-yard races at the track facility on the Southern Methodist University campus. Each runner had someone standing at the finish line, called a "hugger," who embraced the participants as they finished. Before each race Johnny would say to me, "Pop, are you going to yell 'Run, Johnny, run?' "

Whenever the race started I'd be standing on the sidelines yelling at the top of my lungs, "Run, Johnny, run!" I'd get down as close as I could to the track, and I couldn't believe how loud I yelled and carried on when Johnny was racing. It really didn't make any difference how he finished. Everyone got a medal.

During one of Johnny's events I watched the marshals who were running the meet bring out a long rope with a small plastic circle that went around the rope. Then they led the young runner to the rope and let him hold on to the ring. As the ring slipped down the rope the runner would run straight. I was trying to figure out why he held on to a rope, and then I understood: not only was the participant mentally disabled, he was also blind! When he suddenly tripped and fell, every single runner stopped to comfort him and make sure he was all right. Only when the young man got up did they all resume the race.

Over the years the Special Olympics gave Johnny an opportunity to be associated with great people and with all kinds of sporting events, and he also got some much needed exercise. Eventually, he began participating in Frisbee and softball events and branched out into golf and bowling. Johnny always had a great deal of natural ability and a strong sense of wanting to achieve, and watching him enter in these events simply reinforced what I already knew about him.

One afternoon in early January of 1983 Coach Bryant called, and one of the first questions he asked me was "How is Johnny?" He had retired just a few weeks earlier, and as I bragged about how well Johnny had done in the Special Olympics, I thought how the announcement of Coach Bryant's retirement had surprised and saddened his fans. He had never had very much time for small talk, yet that day he kept asking me questions about Johnny, and I knew that if he was asking he sincerely wanted to know about him. Finally, we talked a little about his golf game and how he hoped to be playing more. He said maybe we could get together soon for a round or two of golf. But that was not to happen.

A few weeks later, on January 26, 1983, Coach Bryant died of a heart attack, only a month after he retired. The night before, he had been admitted to Druid City Hospital, where Johnny was born, with chest pains, but no one thought he was in danger. Linda Knowles, Coach Bryant's secretary, whom I had known for years, called to tell me the sad news. I was the first person she told.

"I didn't want you to hear this on the radio or the TV," she said.

I couldn't believe what she was saying and I asked Linda to repeat the news. It was the furthest thing from my mind, and I was too shocked to speak. Finally, I asked Linda if Mrs. Bryant was all right. After I hung up I sat at my desk, put my head in my hands, and cried for a long while. Then I pulled myself together and went to the various coaches' offices and told them all the news. They, too, were stunned. Like me, they all had enormous respect for Coach Bryant. We all thought that he would live forever.

Although he was only seventy years old, he really hadn't been in good health for the past year. Three years before his death he had suffered mild heart failure, and I remembered how I had called him, concerned and worried. He had been in a good mood and told me not to be too upset because he would take his medicine and be fine. Then, a year later, a small blood clot broke loose from his heart and caused a mild stroke. But once again he took his medicine and he was okay. I think few people were aware that he had health problems. He didn't talk about them much.

Now Linda was recounting the days and details leading up to his death. On Tuesday, January 25, he had been visiting Jimmy Hinton, his close friend, when he had a sudden attack of nausea and chest pains that struck him around 6 P.M. He went right to Druid City Hospital. Linda said no one seemed terribly concerned when he was admitted. The report to the news media had come out that he was resting comfortably and that his stay would be short. But twenty-four hours later he was dead of a cardiac arrest.

The funeral, in Tuscaloosa, was emblematic of his legend. The main services were in the First United Methodist Church. The church was packed, and down the street two other churches, the First Baptist Church and the First Presbyterian Church, were filled with University of Alabama trustees and school officials and the general public — an estimated ten thousand people gathered for his funeral in the three churches connected by special audio hookup. The whole town, and for that matter the entire state, mourned. Flags were flown at half-staff; people stood around the streets and sidewalks, huddling in shocked silence. Thousands of people lined the streets as the procession of over three hundred cars passed. Following the services, probably the longest funeral procession in the history of Tuscaloosa (his hearse was followed by buses carrying hundreds of past and present players and dignitaries from all over the United States) passed from downtown, where the streets were blocked off on Tenth Avenue, through the town to the Elmwood Cemetery in Birmingham. I later read in newspapers that many people actually camped out at the cemetery to attend the graveside services.

Coach Bryant always spoke with authority. When he said something you knew he meant it. He was concerned about his players and his staff members and was always gentle in tough situations when dealing with people. I loved the way that he could deal so effectively with his staff, the players, the media, and the alumni. His players weren't just numbers to him because all of the people who played for him felt the same way about him; they sensed they were special to him. He had a way of making each player feel important, and there were many times I wished that I could have dealt with people and situations exactly the way he did, but obviously this was impossible. Ultimately, you have to coach with your own personality, and there was no way I could do things the way Coach Bryant did. But I never stopped trying. Over the years when I would go through some difficult periods dealing with Johnny's disabilities, I'd often sit back and think, "How would Coach Bryant have handled this?" And after a while I'd always have a little more courage.

CHAPTER 8

▼

CARDINAL YEARS

PERHAPS it was the combination of Coach Bryant's death and the fact that my fiftieth birthday was just two years away that made me realize just how much I wanted a head coaching position in the NFL. I had the experience and had put in my time as an assistant coach, and I knew I was qualified, yet I was seeing a lot of other people get jobs before I did. Since 1980 three Cowboy coaching assistants had all gotten head coaching positions in the pros: Dan Reeves had gone to the Denver Broncos, Mike Ditka to the Chicago Bears, and John Mackovic to the Kansas City Chiefs.

Newspaper accounts speculated that if and when Coach Landry retired there was the possibility that I would be considered for his job. But I knew that wasn't in the cards, because he had just signed a three-year contract. And though I decided to look around, I soon found out that there weren't many job openings available. The year before I had turned down an offer to coach the Birmingham Stallions of the upstart United States Football League, and I had recently rejected a few offers to return to college coaching. The NFL

166

was my goal, but it was looking less and less likely that it would happen for me. When I looked around at the good jobs, I realized that somebody already had most of them.

Finally, I started thinking that maybe it wasn't the end of the world for me if I didn't get a head coaching job in the NFL. I was enjoying working for the best — Tom Landry and Tex Schramm — and my family was happy in Dallas. Maybe it was a good idea for me to stay put.

But I was surprised and pleased when Bill Bidwell, the owner of the St. Louis Cardinals, called me in late December of 1985 and asked if I'd be interested in interviewing for the job as head coach. Our first meeting was at Bidwell's house in St. Louis. I found out that I was one of the first men that he had called about the opening. It became clear to me that he was looking for a coach who had been associated with a winning program and who could help turn his team around. The previous coach, Jim Hanifan, had been fired following the final game that fall. Mr. Bidwell told me that he was going to interview other coaches for the position and then get back to me.

A few weeks went by and I didn't hear from him. I would sit around my office and wait for his call just as I had with Bill Peterson of the Oilers. Of course, I knew that Mr. Bidwell had a reputation for working in mysterious ways and for being difficult, but in spite of it I was still disappointed when he didn't call. I started to think that he had probably offered the job to someone else, and I would listen to all the news reports and read everything I could in the paper to see if the Cardinals job had been filled. Finally, I read that Jim Sweeney, the coach of Fresno State, had surfaced as the leading candidate for the job. I found out that he was offered a contract but that he had made a number of demands and was unable to reach an agreement with the Cardinals.

Mr. Bidwell phoned me at home around four o'clock on a Saturday afternoon in February and said, "Hello, is this Gene Stallings? Well, I'm happy to tell you that I'm talking to the new head coach of the St. Louis Cardinals!" I was ecstatic. There were only twenty-eight teams then in the National Football League and he was offering me a head coaching post! He came down to Dallas the next evening and finalized the deal. Now, all of those frustrating moments, the highs of thinking I would surely get the job and lows of waiting and seeing that he had chosen someone else, had come to an end. He came out to our house, completely unannounced, carting a sack of Cardinals souvenirs with him for Johnny — team hats, buttons, pennants, and wristbands. Ruth Ann and I took him out to dinner and while we sat there eating the reality of the situation hit me. I knew that there were few men past age fifty who were offered these kinds of positions. It was a dream fulfilled, and I was celebrating something that I had wanted badly for years.

However, it would be hard for me to stay optimistic for long in my new position as head coach of the Cardinals. Shortly after I arrived, St. Louis sportswriter Bernie Miklasz summed up the situation: "Stallings went from mystique in Dallas to misery in St. Louis, going from a Cowboys organization that never suffered a losing season during his time there to a Cardinals team that never won a playoff game in the NFL. The Cowboys organization is run like a corporation compared to the St. Louis Cardinals, which is run like a small business."

The Cowboys had been to several Super Bowls and the Cardinals had never gone. Clint Murchison, the Cowboys owner, had other means of income and he always put money back into the organization. The Cardinals were a family-run organization that depended on some of the franchise's income. Of course, I knew all of these things, but I worked hard not to compare the organizations because I knew that the bottom line was whether I could get the team to win some games. When a new coach takes over it's usually because the team is not winning, and I was the ninth coach since the Cardinals arrived in St. Louis in 1960.

Before the 1985 season, most sportswriters had chosen the Cardinals to win the division championship and to make a run for the Super Bowl, but by the end of the season they had slipped to 5–11. Perhaps I should have known better, but I was convinced that if I went in and did a good job, things would change. The first thing I had to do was hire a staff. Under NFL rules there is a short period of time each season when you can hire a coach from another pro staff, but that window had expired by the time I took over as head coach. So I had to hire people who were looking for jobs or who didn't have jobs, or draw from the college ranks. I wanted to find as many people as I could who had professional experience. In most places the football coach has something to say about what players he wants. But Mr. Bidwell fixed things so that I didn't have anything to do with the draft at all. I kept thinking that eventually I'd have a little say-so in the draft. Instead, we had a scouting department — a staff of people who were in charge of finding good players — and I basically played with who they brought in. There would be times when I would want a certain player and our scouting department would want somebody else. I was immediately fighting for my coaching career, struggling to win some games and win over the team's front office.

There were other strikes against us because people in St. Louis weren't very supportive of the football Cardinals since they weren't a winning team. It was the baseball Cardinals who got all the respect. Making the disparity more obvious, the two teams used the same facility for practices, which also created a difficult situation. The baseball Cardinals had gone to the World Series the year before, but it had been a long time since the football Cardinals had been in the playoffs.

The sudden move had been tough on Ruth Ann, Martha Kate,

and Johnny. The older girls were either married or off at college. But for Martha Kate, a junior in high school, it was extremely difficult to leave behind lifelong friends — some of whom she had gone to kindergarten with — in the middle of a school year. It wasn't until later that we found out that she cried herself to sleep every night for the first six months that we lived in St. Louis. After a period of time she started to feel accepted at Parkway Central High School. She had a lovely voice and became active in the theater, performing in musicals, which helped her find her place.

We moved into a hotel at first and lived there for a few weeks. My time was immediately consumed with working, and I was obsessed with getting the team up a notch, trying to put a staff together, getting an off-season training program started and enlarging the weight room. Thus, all domestic duties fell to Ruth Ann, and it was her job to find a house to rent, which she soon did. We rented from an elderly couple who spent a great deal of time on Cape Cod. Of course, the house came furnished, but it was an odd feeling to be using someone else's linens, silverware, and furniture. In the spring the owners abruptly came back and Ruth Ann had to scramble to find another house. Fortunately she found a rental diagonally across the street from where we had been living, and a few Saturdays later, Ruth Ann, Martha Kate, Johnny, and I lugged armloads of clothes and our other personal belongings into it. We really didn't have enough stuff to hire a moving van. Johnny had graduated from school in Dallas and gone on to work at a workshop there. Now for the first time in fourteen years, he had no place to go, and we weren't comfortable leaving him by himself. Every time Ruth Ann went out, even if it was just around the corner to mail a letter, Johnny had to go with her.

But we realized that we had turned a very important corner over the last fourteen years and were no longer worried about being accepted because of Johnny. In fact, that was the last thing on our mind. We were far more concerned that he make friends and have a meaningful place to go each day to work. He had had such a positive experience going to church in Dallas, and when we left the congregation they had a going-away party just for him. But now when we took him to church in St. Louis he was unusually reserved and always sat with us. After the service was over people would come over and talk to Ruth Ann and me, but few people would engage him. One Sunday after church the minister came over to Johnny and said that someone had left a gift with his name on it. We went to the back of the church and there was a large brightly wrapped present sitting on a table. We read the gift tag with Johnny's name. He tore open the present to find a big brown stuffed bear with a red ribbon tied around its neck. He buried his face in the bear's fur and squeezed it tight. We looked all over to find another card that might have told us who the gift came from, but we could find no other information. The next Sunday the minister stopped us as we were leaving church and said there was another gift for Johnny and handed him a large basket of fruit. Once again, there was no card on the basket. Each Sunday another gift would appear in the back of the church, and this continued for several more months. Now Johnny couldn't wait to get to church on Sundays, and when the word got out among the parishioners that he was the recipient of mysterious packages, everyone wanted to meet him. We never did find out who was responsible for the presents.

Even though St. Louis was a smaller city than Dallas, it was the largest city in Missouri, and we were happy with the schools and the excellent cultural activities that we could take advantage of. We thought we'd be in St. Louis for a long time, and once again we decided to build a house. This time we built a Southern colonial with green shutters on a pretty lot in a new development. While the house was being built Ruth Ann found a job program for people with disabilities called the Lafayette program and she enrolled

Johnny. Although we knew that it wouldn't be as stimulating as working at the funeral home had been, it was a place for him to go and meet other people his age. He called the program his "school," because he watched Martha Kate going off to school every day and heard her talk about all her friends and activities.

When Johnny had graduated from CTC, in Dallas, just three years earlier, at age twenty-one, I remembered sitting in the auditorium watching as he and his classmates went up onstage in caps and gowns and received diplomas. At times throughout his childhood, I had hoped that he would one day learn to read so well that he'd be able to sit down and grasp an entire book. I thought maybe he'd be able to add and subtract numbers, too. But as his name was called and he walked across the stage and shook hands with the principal that evening, I knew that he would never be able to read more than a few street signs and that he could only identify some numbers. Maybe we could have pushed him harder to learn, but we had always taken great care not to set him up for disappointment; it just wouldn't have been worth it. Early on we had decided against putting a lot of pressure on him.

Still, I knew he had the potential to do something more challenging. All you had to do is try and beat him at a game of Memory, where the aim was to remember where each card was on the table and match it with its mate. Nearly every time, he'd turn over the right cards. Or you'd just have to ask him the name of a player I had coached five or ten years before and he'd think for a minute and come up with the right name every time.

I had hoped that St. Louis would be able to offer Johnny something a little different in terms of work and that maybe there would be something special there where he could use his talents. But we soon found out that no one in the new program was his age, and the work that he was doing there was mundane — sealing envelopes and putting things in bags. It bothered me that my twenty-four-year-old son wasn't being challenged more. Even though he seemed perfectly content when I'd go out to visit him, I could tell that he was bored. He would occasionally fall asleep or just stop working in the middle of a project. I had seen his animated smile and enthusiasm while he was working at the funeral home, and I wanted to see him like that now. Still, we were all glad that he had a place to go every day.

It was obvious that the best part of Johnny's week was attending Saturday practices with me. Every Friday night before the next day's practice, as he was getting ready for bed he'd say, "Pop, don't forget to wake me up." But, I never had to worry about that. At 5 A.M. he would be standing at my bedroom door, fully dressed and ready to go! And before we'd leave the house he'd put on his Cardinals shirt with "HEAD TRAINER" printed on the front, a present from his sisters when we moved to St. Louis. Whenever anyone asked him about the shirt he'd say, "I'm the Cardinals' trainer." In fact, Johnny's closet was crammed full of Cardinals shirts, caps, and sweaters given to him by Mr. Bidwell. From the beginning, he allowed Johnny to fly with him on the team plane, even though it was always crowded with media and other people wanting to travel with us. Johnny really missed his Cowboys friends like Roger Staubach, Cliff Harris, and Charlie Waters, but right away he started memorizing the Cardinals players' names and striking up friendships with many of them. Pretty soon Johnny started thinking that the Cardinals were his very own team. As soon as we'd get to the locker room, Johnny would go looking for J. T. Smith, our wide receiver, because he'd always have a doughnut for him. During the practice he'd stand over with me at the sidelines and as the Cardinals would come off the field, he'd give each of them a high five. Neil Lomax, our quarterback, and LeBaron Caruthers, our strength and conditioning coach, played cards with Johnny every Saturday. They would divide up the cards in their simple game, turn one up, and if Johnny had a six and LeBaron had a five, Johnny would win. They patiently played that game for hours and they'd always let Johnny win. Neil liked to play catch with Johnny out on the field and he always acted like he had all the time in the world for him.

After we had been in St. Louis about a month we were invited to our first dinner party by the Bucks. I sat next to Carol Buck, whose husband was the announcer of the St. Louis Cardinals baseball team. Carol was involved in a million activities and was well known in St. Louis. She had a radio show and interviewed the wives of Cardinals players. She and I talked about our children and I learned that she had a son and daughter, and then I found myself talking about Johnny and worrying out loud about how hard it was for him to meet new friends. The next afternoon Carol came over to the house with a tape for Johnny of *The King and I.* I could tell how pleased he was that night when Ruth Ann told me about Carol's visit. A few weeks later she drove over in her red Corvette convertible and took Johnny for a ride, and pretty soon she started doing this once a week. We later found out that she had performed on Broadway when she was younger.

Carol provided Johnny with hours of entertainment, but Ruth Ann and I wished that there were other young people his age, in their twenties, that Johnny could be friends with. He was so dependent on Martha Kate, and we worried that he'd be devastated when she went to college. She had recently been in the musical *Fiddler on the Roof,* and Johnny went to see it about four or five times. In fact, he knew all her lines and songs. I thought about the game that Johnny and Martha Kate had made up and constantly played called Trust Me. They would be out in the backyard, taking turns standing one behind the other and falling backward, each trusting the other to catch him or her at the last minute.

Although the family was settling into life in St. Louis, I was exhausted, frustrated, and irritable by the end of a 4–11–1 season in 1986. I loved being a head coach and being in charge of a team, but tension was mounting between Mr. Bidwell and me as the losses piled up. I worked for him and it was my responsibility to please him, but I was having a hard time adapting to his manner and I spoke out when I wasn't happy with certain situations. More than anything I wanted to get the team up and winning. I'm sure that there were times when the players felt I was too demanding. I knew they were working hard and they had clearly shown me that they were loyal, yet I continued to be hard on them because I hated to lose and I wasn't used to finishing in last place. I was so obsessed with winning that I pushed them hard — much harder than I should have.

That June, Ruth Ann, Johnny, Martha Kate, and I headed to the farm for a much needed break. We hadn't been there more than a few days when Mario Pelligrini, the producer and director of all of the United Way spots on television, called and asked if he could meet with me. "Coach Stallings, we'd like for you to do a spot for us. Do you have any involvement with a charity, or perhaps a personal situation we might be able to use for a spot?"

"Yes, I have a son who has Down syndrome," I said.

The next week Mario came down to the farm. I instantly liked his warm and approachable manner. He told me that early in his career he had directed feature films. But his life changed in the 1960s when his wife died unexpectedly of leukemia. After coping with that difficult experience he went to the American Cancer Society and produced a strong antismoking spot that featured the actor Yul Brynner, who was dying of lung cancer. The tobacco companies, who were big advertisers in broadcasting, tried to prevent the spot from running, but it eventually made it on the air and the public's response was very positive. These "service" spots had been shown on every NFL game telecast for the last ten years and featured NFL players involved in community projects and charities funded by the United Way.

"It would be a great thing if you could come on the air for all of the parents who have that situation, to show how you've coped with it," said Mario. "But, it's going to take a lot of courage. Eighty million people are going to see you, and you are going to present your son. Are you really sure you want to do this?"

"Yes, I want to do this," I answered back right away. I hadn't discussed the commercial with anyone, but then I started thinking about what I had agreed to do and realized that our family might be too exposed. I wondered how the commercial might affect Johnny. I went back and forth for a few days, and finally I thought back to how I had talked with parents in Dallas who had children who were born with Down syndrome and how they had contacted me looking for support. It had been comforting knowing that there were other people out there who were going through some of the same struggles we were, and I was always surprised by how much support and strength we gave each other.

Johnny and I filmed the commercial outside St. Louis on a farm that was supposed to look like ours in Paris. As we drove out into the countryside, he and I talked a little bit about the commercial, and I could see that he was getting kind of excited. He wanted to do it right and he was afraid that he might fall off of his horse with the camera rolling. Mario didn't tell us what we were supposed to do until we arrived at the farm.

When we got there Mario greeted us and started the ball rolling. He handed me a script and told me to go off with Johnny and rehearse for a little while. Johnny and I settled down by a big oak tree, and I read my lines out loud and told him where Mario wanted him to stand. When we went back to find Mario we saw that there were people set up to brush our hair and put makeup on us. It took us a few times to get it right and Johnny and I laughed when we messed up our lines. In the commercial we started out filming inside a small house, and I face the camera and say, "I've coached some of the greatest athletes in the NFL and I know the rewards of victory."

Then I point to a picture of Johnny with me that's on the wall in back of us. "But none has been as important to me as working with this young man, John. When he was born, he was diagnosed with having Down syndrome. In some ways he would never be like other children. For him, there will never be a chance to play in the National Football League."

Then the film shows Johnny working on a leather bracelet, which is the kind of activity that he had been doing at the Lafayette program. He is slowly stamping out the letters "D-A-D." Then I say, "Over the years I've seen him grow. He's twenty-four years old now. His progress is measured in little victories.

"The times we spend together are very special to me," I say as the camera focuses on Johnny and me. I put the bracelet on his wrist. "John made this for me with a great deal of love. The same kind of love I have for him. For, you see, John is my son. When you support the United Way, you're saying to people like John, 'Don't give up. We'll give you a helping hand. You can make it.' "

The filming of the commercial took most of the day, and by the time we got in the car and headed back to St. Louis it was getting dark. As we passed miles of isolated cornfields and farms, I looked over at Johnny and his face was ashen. "Movie stars always get tired," I told him. "Would the movie star like to go out to a restaurant and eat tonight?"

"Yes, Pop. The movie star would like to eat out," Johnny said. We stopped at a roadside diner and had a hamburger. Then we got back in the car and continued on home. I turned on the radio and found a baseball game and Johnny put his head on my lap and instantly fell asleep.

In the beginning of the 1987 season the commercial aired during some NFL games. I was surprised at how well produced it was, and unexpectedly I started getting loads of phone calls. Young couples who had recently given birth to children with Down syndrome were calling me, wanting to talk. I found myself speaking with these parents for thirty and forty minutes at a time, and as I listened to their distressed voices and sympathized with their hopelessness, all of the sad feeling that I had experienced twenty-five years before when Johnny was diagnosed with Down syndrome came back to haunt me.

That season Joe Browne, the NFL's director of communications, said it was one of the most popular spots in the history of the league's United Way series, and the NFL decided to rerun the commercial the next season. Suddenly people started recognizing Johnny and me in airports and other public places, which sometimes gave me an uneasy feeling because many times total strangers wanted to talk. Since they had seen us on television a number of times they felt we were old friends. But as time passed, I became more accustomed to this and I realized that for many people it was their first exposure to a person with Down syndrome.

The filming of the commercial had been a high point in an otherwise difficult first year with the Cardinals. When I returned to St. Louis from the farm I vowed that during the 1987 season I would pull back a little with the players and be less demanding during practices. On the other hand I was more determined than ever to prove that I could turn the team into a consistent winner, and I put in longer hours than I ever had. But on the second day of practice I read in the newspapers that the team might be moving. That afternoon I asked Mr. Bidwell about the news reports, and he just shrugged. He was known for keeping people off guard, and now suddenly in the beginning of the second season the coaches and players were unsure as to whether we were going to move or not. Things were in turmoil. We found out later in the season that there were several cities courting the Cardinals, Phoenix being one of them.

That fall our team did fairly well, but we still didn't get into the playoffs and there was constant speculation about whether we were going to Baltimore or Phoenix. In March, when the season was over, Ruth Ann and I went to Phoenix for a league meeting, and finally one afternoon while we were there Mr. Bidwell called us in and told us that the team was moving to Phoenix. It was hard for us to grasp that we were actually going to leave St. Louis. We started looking for a house that very weekend, and as we drove around the city with a real estate broker we couldn't get used to yards without grass, trees, or flowers. The desert was new to us, and although we found there was a certain beauty to the barren landscape, we missed the green countryside of St. Louis. After looking at at least thirty stucco houses, we finally bought a California-style house with a tile roof and a lap pool in the backyard. We chose it because it backed up to a lush golf course. After Martha Kate graduated from high school in June, we headed off to Phoenix.

Although Phoenix was a city anxious to have its own NFL team and welcomed us with open arms, and though I was excited about the move, it was frustrating uprooting Johnny and Ruth Ann once again and trying to sell a brand-new house that we had lived in for only fourteen months. At least Martha Kate would be going away to college in Texas and we didn't have to worry about taking her out of yet another school.

In June the team started off with a camp at an abandoned high school in Phoenix. The players weren't used to the searing dry heat that rose to 110 degrees and higher most days. Neil Lomax's feet were swollen and sore and he had a hard time running. Stump Mitchell, our running back, got too much sun one day and nearly passed out. The players weren't the only ones suffering from the heat. From the minute we got there we could see that Johnny was having a harder time than usual getting his breath and he was moving around a lot slower. We heard about a workshop outside of Phoenix that was similar to the Lafayette program in St. Louis. But,

179

Johnny's slow pace and his gasping for breath worried us and we decided he was better off not exerting himself because anything he did seemed to take great effort. But I knew Johnny would have liked working and meeting new people at a workshop, and I think he was frustrated that we held him back.

He spent every Wednesday with Howard Olsen, who had built our swimming pool in Phoenix years before. Johnny went with Howard to work and visited lots of houses where there were swimming pools. They liked each other and Johnny begged us to let him spend more time with Howard, but we had grown more and more concerned about Johnny's health and kept him home most days. I often felt guilty about moving the family so much, and I wondered if Johnny would have had more friends his age if we had stayed in one place.

Johnny started having severe stomachaches, and we soon found out that he had a double hernia. The doctors said that he had to be operated on, but they assured us that the anesthesia was easier to regulate now than when he was a child and that he wouldn't be in danger. But there was no reassuring me. I was convinced something terrible would happen in surgery. On the day of his scheduled surgery the scorching heat from the streets seemed to follow us inside the hospital, and as they put Johnny on a stretcher I felt numb from worrying. But Johnny showed little concern and as he talked and joked with the nurses, he relieved some of our anxiety. The surgery was short and Johnny handled it well and came home the next day.

Just as soon as he was able, he and Ruth Ann began to swim in our pool, which looked out to the golf course, almost every afternoon, after the temperature outside had cooled off a little. It was so hot every day that he had to stay inside most of the time, so by the end of the day he couldn't wait to jump in the pool. He never learned to swim, but he could bounce from side to side, which kept us from worrying about him too much if our backs were turned for an instant.

Johnny missed Martha Kate terribly. He carried her picture in his wallet, and when she called he would often go into his room and cry after they spoke on the telephone. She missed him, too, and when she would come home from college, she would usually bring friends with her and they would take Johnny on outings and spend all of their time with him. Several of her friends ended up teaching children with special needs and have told us over the years that Johnny was the reason they chose their field. Later, when Martha Kate became a teacher, the children with Down's were always placed in her classroom.

Once again, I found myself going into Johnny's room in the middle of every night to make sure that he was breathing. In the dark, I'd sit on a chair next to his bed and watch him lying there, all buttoned up in his red pajamas, his mouth wide open, trying hard to suck in air while making strange noises, his chest heaving up and down, and I'd think to myself how I wouldn't want to do very much if I had to gasp for my breath the way Johnny did. It seemed just like yesterday that he was that little boy whose days were so precarious. He had struggled for his breath for twenty-six years, yet somehow his body had adjusted. But now as I sat there and looked at him, I wondered how much longer he could possibly go on like this. I put my ear to his chest so that I would hear his heartbeat, just as I had done throughout his childhood, and I thought how much I'd like to have my son's courage and determination, particularly during this juncture in my life.

Our first season in Phoenix was full of ups and downs. We had victories over three teams who were recent Super Bowl champions — the New York Giants, Washington, and San Francisco. In fact, we had a 7–4 start and people were talking like we'd go to the playoffs. But then we had a trying loss to Cincinnati and then five consecutive losses that of course dashed any hopes for the playoffs. We had a rash of injuries and didn't start the same team two weeks in a row. Mr. Bidwell and I hardly spoke during the season.

That next spring the director for the Genetics Research Center of Scottsdale approached me and asked if the Cardinals would be interested in participating in a program called First Down for Down Syndrome. The idea was that corporate and individual sponsors would be asked to match dollars or cents for Cardinals first downs during the regular season. Based on team productivity over the last few years, we estimated that about 325 first downs would be made in 1989. A core of corporate sponsors including McDonald's Corporation, a local news channel, and America West Airlines helped launch the program. The money that was raised would be used for researching the cure for Down syndrome. Even if we didn't raise a lot of money, I thought the program would raise awareness about Down syndrome. But the idea caught on fast, and pretty soon people, companies, organizations, and individuals from all over the state were pledging from fifty cents to five or ten dollars for each first down.

We brought Christopher Burke to Phoenix to help us raise money and bring more awareness to the First Down for Down Syndrome program. Chris played Corky Thacher in the television series *Life Goes On,* which had just premiered on ABC. The idea of having someone with Down syndrome portraying a character with Down's was bold and daring. Chris quickly gained the public's interest and attention. He had a vibrant personality and when I was with him I felt like I was with a celebrity. He arrived with an entourage of people and he ran out to the field with Johnny and watched football practice. After a while I asked Chris and Johnny if I could take them out to dinner. We went to an outdoor restaurant that had a dance floor, and while the three of us were sitting there eating the manager came up to me and asked if he could make a little introduction. He then announced Chris Burke from the show *Life Goes On.* Chris stood up, took the mike, and said he was delighted to be there with his good friend Coach Gene Stallings and his son,

182

Johnny. Then he and Johnny hit the dance floor. The two of them danced and carried on until I finally had to tell them it was time to go.

The second season in Phoenix, 1989, was not much different from the first. We were always a step or two away from achieving more wins than losses, and I thought I was doing a good job. But then we had eighteen starting players miss at least one game because of injuries. Nevertheless, we were still competitive, and I felt as though we were in the thick of things and we'd finally get to the playoffs.

My contract was to expire at the end of the year. When Larry Wilson, the general manager of the team, was approached about renewing my contract, he said he wanted to see me coach another game. Then I read a story in the *St. Louis Post Dispatch* in which Wilson expressed aggravation about my popularity among the Cardinals' fans and the media. Wilson was quoted as saying that I worked at being popular. I was troubled by his statement and by the way I was being scrutinized. Of course, I had been coaching football long enough to know that the success of a team depends on many coaches and players, and I was fully aware that one man doesn't make the show. I decided that I had to set up a meeting with Wilson on November 18, the night before we played the Los Angeles Rams, hoping to resolve our differences. But it accomplished nothing, and I left the meeting feeling frustrated and dissatisfied. The next day the Rams beat us 37–14.

I think the decision not to renew my contract had already been made, and I had heard rumors that Wilson was looking for my replacement well before our meeting. Obviously, that made me think that he was not going to renew my contract. So I held a press conference in which I said, "I plan to fulfill my contract. There's no question about that. However, I will not seek to have my contract renewed." I thought that by saying this I could end speculation about my job, and end the distractions surrounding the Cardinals. I could then spend all my efforts trying to get the team into the playoffs. I figured that the attention should be on the team, not on me. So when I said I wouldn't be returning I thought I was doing them a favor. I figured I'd get the team over the hump and after the season was over I'd step aside and they would bring in a new coach.

But Wilson had different ideas than I did. He feared it would be unsettling if I remained with the team through the final weeks of the season. He fired me the next day and appointed running backs coach Hank Kuhlman as interim head coach. The Cardinals lost the next six games.

Two days after I was fired, I was clearing out my office and I requested to meet with the team one last time and give them some encouragement. But Wilson turned me down. Mr. Bidwell never spoke to me while my future was being decided or after my dismissal. I sat on the floor of my office and taped up the last packing box, and as I carried it out into the hall I saw Johnny and Ruth Ann walking toward me. When Johnny saw me, he broke away from Ruth Ann, walked quickly down the hall, and gave me a hug. "It's okay, Pop," he said and patted me on the back.

When we had first arrived in Phoenix, my mother, Nell, at age eighty-eight, was asked to make a commercial for a local bank about saving money. She thought it sounded like fun and she is shown sitting in a rocking chair as the words "Nell," then "Nell Stallings" flash across the screen. As she rocks some more "Nell Stallings, mother of Coach Gene Stallings" flashes across the screen. Then my mother says, "I told my little boy one of these days there was going to be an emergency and he better save his money." Then they show my mother turning to me and saying, "Now isn't mother always right?"

As soon as the bank found out that I was fired, they came in and said, "Coach, would you please do one more commercial for us?" I agreed, reluctantly, because it meant staying in Phoenix two days longer than I had wanted. But once I got to the studio, I found that I got a certain pleasure out of saying my lines.

On the new commercial I said, "My mother told me I should save my money, so I started a savings program that paid me good interest rates and lets me get to my money when I need it, and I need it now." Then I smiled and said, "You never know when one of these little emergencies will come up."

The very next day Johnny, Ruth Ann, and I drove twenty-two hours straight through to the farm, which has always been there as a refuge for us. I desperately needed to pull in my reins and do some serious thinking about my future as well as the family's. I was a fifty-four-year-old coach who had been fired twice, and now I felt more than ever that I needed to protect us all, and the farm was the perfect place to do that. It was one place that never seemed to change. I could sit in my rocking chair on the screened-in porch of the cabin, work out in the bucolic meadows with Mr. Henry, or take a walk with my family, and I'd always gain a little perspective on things. But unlike when I was fired at A&M, the minute I set foot inside the cabin the phone started ringing.

Roger Staubach called to see if I was interested in becoming a coach at Navy. I told him I was hesitant about going so far away from my girls and from my parents, who were getting older. I was really torn because I loved the Naval Academy. Roger finally persuaded me to let him set up an interview there for me. While I was interviewing in Annapolis I read in the newspaper that Bill Curry had surprisingly resigned from Alabama to become the head coach at Kentucky.

I sincerely wanted to be at Alabama, but I never thought I'd get another chance. I've always loved the Alabama people because of their great tradition and spirit, and I wanted to continue the winning ways that Coach Bryant had established. In twenty-five seasons at Alabama he had compiled a 232–46–9 record and taken the team to twenty-four consecutive bowl games. He won six national championships as head coach and thirteen SEC titles. Of course there were other great coaches, like Wallace Wade, in the 1920s, and later Frank Thomas, who coached the Tide to two national championships and four SEC titles. But Coach Bryant was the standard by which all Alabama coaches would always be measured.

Dr. Roger Sayers, the president of the University of Alabama, called to set up an interview, and he and Hootie Ingram, the athletic director, flew out to Paris. I could tell that they wanted me to make a decision pretty quickly, because I'm sure there were many coaches who would have loved to have the job. It turned out to be a blessing that I was fired from the Cardinals at Thanksgiving because if I had finished out the NFL year the Alabama job would have been filled.

I accepted their offer on the spot, thrilled to have one of the premier jobs in college football. I was going to the place where I had started my career and would now most likely end it. It was a dream fulfilled, and it had been offered to me at a perfect time in my life and, as it turned out, a perfect time in Johnny's life.

CHAPTER 9

TRANSFORMED IN
TUSCALOOSA

ON January 10, 1990, Ruth Ann and I flew into Tuscaloosa from the farm, stopping off in Dallas to leave Johnny with Jackie and her husband, John Chalk, for the first few days until we got a little more settled. The next day I was introduced as the head coach of Alabama at a midmorning press conference at the university's state-of-the-art football complex. As I walked in the front door and looked around, I was impressed by the indoor practice field and large beautiful offices, all new since I had last coached at Alabama. A number of former Crimson Tide players and coaches (among them Bart Starr and Lee Roy Jordan) had come to show their support, and I was happy to see them. Afterward Coach Bryant's son, Paul Jr., a businessman in Tuscaloosa, embraced me and said, "This is what Papa would have wanted." I had been dreaming about this moment for years.

Over at the university, the student population had almost doubled in size and was now twenty thousand. Even though many new buildings had sprung up on the campus, it still had the feel of the lovely, gracious campus built over a hundred years ago. But downtown Tuscaloosa, which had been the center of the commercial traffic when I was coaching at Alabama in the sixties, seemed unusually quiet and tired. These days people shopped and congregated at the malls along Highway 82.

When I had first come to the university in 1958, the athletic department was housed along with other departments in an old building called Moore Hall. There was an ancient gymnasium on the top floor and the offices were small and dimly lit. In fact, Coach Bryant's office had once been a big team shower and it was the only office with carpet. But as a twenty-three-year-old fresh out of college, I thought the facilities were just fine.

When I drove my usual route to work and glanced up at the street signs I noticed that Tenth Avenue had been renamed Bryant Drive. Denny Stadium, which had been named after George Denny, the university's longtime president, was now called Bryant-Denny Stadium. And a state-of-the-art museum devoted entirely to the history of Alabama football, had become one of college football's most famous attractions, the Paul "Bear" Bryant Museum. Next door and across the street from the football complex, there was a large modern conference center also named after Coach Bryant.

One afternoon when I drove past Druid City Hospital, I had a vivid memory of leaving the large brick complex the day after Johnny was born there twenty-seven years before. It was dark when I had left Ruth Ann and Johnny and had pulled out onto University Boulevard, forgetting to turn my headlights on. A man driving a tractor-trailer truck flashed his lights to signal that mine were off. But I was so distracted that I didn't react. It wasn't until he blasted his horn that I responded and turned on the lights. I had looked over at the remaining cigars with the blue bands sitting in their wooden box on the seat beside me, and I pulled into a gas station and dumped them into a trash can. When I arrived home that night the girls came running down the stairs in their pajamas. I remembered the excited look they had in their eyes when they asked me about their new brother.

Meanwhile there had been big improvements at Partlow State School and Hospital, the state institution for mentally retarded youngsters, which had operated under a federal court order for fifteen years from 1972 to 1986. Overcrowding was no longer a problem. I found out that in 1981 the Alabama state legislature passed a $15 million bond issue that allowed for new construction and renovation. Now there were newer, more modern facilities in back of the older buildings, and the residents who had sat outside around the fountain rocking back and forth had disappeared.

Ruth Ann flew back to Dallas to get Johnny, and we stayed at the Sheraton Capstone Hotel on the campus until our house was ready. From the minute we arrived at the hotel, all of the staff — the bellman, desk people, maids, and concierge — seemed to be familiar with Johnny and were especially nice to him. Many of them mentioned how they had seen him on the United Way commercial. In fact, I was surprised at how many people around town had seen that commercial. People would stop Johnny on the streets of Tuscaloosa, greet him warmly, and want to carry on a conversation with him. The staff at the hotel allowed us to break the rules and keep Boo Boo, his cat, in our hotel suite, and they brought Johnny candy and little gifts, trying to make him feel that for the few months we were there this was his home.

Johnny seemed to smile constantly from all the attention he was receiving, and it made me feel good, too. I thought how lucky Ruth Ann and I were at our ages to have our son by our side. One of the toughest parts of parenthood for me had always been letting go of my girls. Every time one of them went off to college or got married, I felt sad. And of course Johnny was always by my side and shared my sadness. It had been tough on Johnny to have his sisters leave home, too. But now that the girls have had children and Johnny has become an uncle, a new dimension has been added to all of our lives.

When Laurie was pregnant with her second child she didn't know whether she was going to have a girl or a boy — if she was to have a girl she would name the baby Jacklyn; if a boy, John Mark. On June 23, 1991, the whole family was waiting for the news at the hospital and everybody — the hospital staff, our friends and family — knew that if it was a boy it would be named John Mark. Johnny stood outside the delivery room chanting, "Boy, boy, boy!" I paced nervously up and down the halls, wondering what in the world we were going to do if the baby was a girl. Finally they wheeled Laurie out to where we were standing and she was holding the little baby all wrapped up in a blanket and she looked at Johnny and said, "Oh, Johnny, it's a boy, it's a John Mark!"

Tears streamed down his cheeks and he said, "Thank you, my sister, thank you, my brother, Good job, Doc." And at that moment I was never more thrilled to have a grandson.

Anna Lee had two little girls and Laurie had an older son. They all followed Johnny around wherever he went. He would play their games with them, and whether it was "house," hide-and-seek, or "go fish," didn't seem to matter. They would bring all of their little friends over to the house to meet Johnny, and there was never any kind of hesitation or embarrassment among any of the children when they met "Uncle Johnny." The only time Johnny would become annoyed with them was if they messed up his room or didn't put his tapes away in the correct case.

Of course, as the years have passed I have worried a great deal about what is going to happen to Johnny. It is a nagging fear and concern that I've carried around all my life, and more so as I have gotten older. I know that all of my girls would love to have him if anything ever happened to Ruth Ann or me. But they have young families and big responsibilities. A few years before we moved to Alabama Ruth Ann and I helped found Disability Resources, in Abilene, Texas, which provides complete care for people with developmental disabilities when their parents can no longer take care of them. I know this is a major concern with many parents who have children with disabilities.

We had only been in Tuscaloosa a few days when basketball coach Wimp Sanderson's wife, Annette, called to invite Johnny and Ruth Ann over. I thought back to the Christmas party at my office when Johnny was six months old and remembered holding the Sandersons' son, Scott, in my arms. I wondered what his life was like now, what kind of work he did, and whether he had ever married. Ruth Ann was thrilled to be reconnecting with Annette, and she and Johnny went over the next day. Annette had changed very little. She was still the hospitable, caring woman that she had always been. She warmly embraced Ruth Ann and Johnny the minute they walked in the door. As she left the room to get refreshments in the kitchen, Ruth Ann studied the various pictures of Scott that sat on the bookshelf and on tables around the room. There was one of him kissing his bride and another snapshot of Scott cradling an infant in his arms.

When Annette came back into the room carrying a tray of Cokes, the doorbell rang and in walked Baila Block and her son, Bradley. Although Ruth Ann had never met them before, right after Johnny was born we were told that another family in Tuscaloosa had had a baby boy with Down syndrome, just six months before. Bradley was that boy.

I think there is something instinctive in the way that Johnny gravitates toward others who have Down's, and the minute he saw Bradley, he walked over to him and gave him a high five. Then the two young men put their arms around each other and disappeared into the other room.

"They're just like two magnets," Baila said as she was introduced to Ruth Ann.

"I've been so anxious for you all to meet," said Annette.

Baila then told Ruth Ann that back in 1962 she had sent what little literature there was at the time on Down syndrome to Ruth Ann, but she had never heard back from her. Ruth Ann, perhaps because she was so distracted at the time, didn't remember receiving the information. She and Baila talked for hours that day about their experiences raising their sons. They commiserated over not being able to communicate with their toddlers and lamented the fact that they knew of no speech or occupational therapists in the early days. As the two of them compared notes, they discovered their sons were on the same level educationally; like Johnny, Bradley had not had any formal schooling until he was about ten years old. Bradley had never learned to read or write fluently and could identify only some numbers. But both boys were very sociable and good athletes. Bradley was able to do more physically because he didn't have a heart defect.

From that day on our boys were inseparable and Johnny wanted to do all of the things that Bradley did. Through the Parks and Recreation Association and the Tuscaloosa Association for Retarded Children Johnny and Bradley went bowling. My sons-in-law had always liked bowling with Johnny and had had a special ball made for him that accommodated his very large clubbed thumb. Johnny started bowling a high score (over one hundred) using a unique style of just dropping the ball and watching it take forever to knock the pins down. He and Bradley would go on golf outings, line dance, and participate in talent shows and outings to "Disney on Ice," in Birmingham, the Grand Ole Opry, in Nashville, and to museums, restaurants, and amusement parks. There were still times when Johnny's speech created a barrier with some people. But Bradley and he never had trouble understanding each other. It was almost as if they shared a common language.

Through their social activities, Johnny started meeting more friends, and soon he was inviting them over to our house to sleep over on Saturday nights. I could never have imagined how much fun it would be for Ruth Ann and me to once again host slumber parties. Johnny and his friends would do all of the typical things a teenager would do. They'd eat pizza, listen to CDs, and dance together or watch reruns of football games until I'd have to go in and tell them to turn the lights out. Then Ruth Ann would cook a big breakfast for them the next morning, acting like a short-order cook, making pancakes for Bradley, eggs for Johnny, and cereal for another friend.

Bradley always made sure Johnny had his wallet with him when they went out or that he had his tapes and tape player so that they could sing together. Sometimes Johnny would get upset at the way he thought Bradley was "bossing him around." Or at times Bradley would tease Johnny and call him "Johnny wonny."

"Only my Pop can call me that!" he would say.

Johnny finally had a life that was very much independent from Ruth Ann and me. When the telephone rang at our house, many times it would be for him, and he and his friends would make arrangements without any help from us. And although we had thought our days of carpooling were over, we found ourselves once again taking Johnny and his friends from place to place. We couldn't have been more delighted.

Bradley had a job at PALK Enterprises, an organization that provided opportunities for adults with disabilities to make the transition into the workforce. He silk-screened shirts, assembled plaques, packaged products, and cut samples of fabrics and carpet. Although the work was repetitious, very much like what Johnny had been doing over the years, he saw how proud Bradley was of working and earning money, and he was anxious to have a job working alongside his best friend. Ruth Ann took Johnny to the McGraw Center, in Tuscaloosa, where he would be trained to perform a pay-ing job at PALK. Not long afterward, Johnny was working alongside Bradley at PALK every day.

Working at PALK not only provided Johnny with a job, but now he had many new friends from work. I thought back to our days in St. Louis and Phoenix and how lonely he had been with no place to go all day. The "big small town" of Tuscaloosa, with a population of sixty thousand, was the perfect size to meet the needs of its citizens, and there were many people in town who were strong advocates for people with disabilities, developing work and leisure programs. In Tuscaloosa, everyone seemed to know each other, and I soon found out that the parents of children with disabilities had been instrumental in getting their children jobs and helping them create social lives. They also had found out what certain agencies did and what they, as parents of children with disabilities, were entitled to by law, and then they pushed a little. After the Americans with Disabilities Act of 1990 was enacted in 1992, there seemed to be even more of an awareness. The aim of the act was to prohibit discrimination against people with disabilities in housing, transportation, communications, state and local government, construction, and by employers with more than fifteen workers. The federal government did a good job of making people aware of the new laws, yet even today the laws are not always complied with. Unless parents ask for certain programs, the agencies sometimes don't provide them even if they are required by law.

Yet there were so many good activities and job-training opportunities in Tuscaloosa for people Johnny's age that Ruth Ann and I wondered if the town offered any kind of programs for young children with disabilities. It didn't take long for us to learn about the model early-intervention program called RISE, which when it began was an acronym for Rural Infant Stimulation Environment. Not long after we had returned to Tuscaloosa a woman named Betty Shirley, who was very active with RISE, called, asking if Ruth Ann would go down to one of the fraternities and accept a check for the program. She told us that she had seen the United Way commercial and knew about Johnny. Ruth Ann said yes, of course she would accept the check, but when she got up onstage she realized she had no idea what RISE was about. When Betty asked her if there was anything she'd like to say Ruth Ann said no and quickly sat down.

During that time I had been spending my days familiarizing myself with the returning players, and assembling a good staff. One February afternoon I took a break, joined Betty and Ruth Ann, and went over to visit the RISE program in Wilson Hall on central campus, which had been the women's dormitory, just twenty-five feet across the alleyway from my office back when I was an assistant coach. We walked into the sixty-year-old building and I was so taken aback by what I saw that for a moment I could hardly speak. There were sixty-five children crammed into four small classrooms. The place was literally bursting at the seams; it reminded me of what I had heard Partlow was like back in the 1960s and 70s. But this was the first time RISE had been located in a real building and they thought they had a lot of space.

Right away I noticed the ten or fifteen children who had Down syndrome. Others were in wheelchairs, some had braces on their legs, and many of the children appeared to be much smaller than their age. There were a few children in the classroom who were not disabled, creating an atmosphere of diversity. It must have been close to eighty-five degrees in the building on that mild winter day and I took off my sports jacket and loosened my tie.

As I walked around the classroom, I saw that at least twenty-six teachers and teacher's aides were actively engaged with the children and I watched as they worked on developmental skills with them, patiently training children to walk, talk, use the toilet, and helping them learn to get dressed by themselves. I thought how in tune they were with the children and what a good time they all seemed to be having. Over in the corner of one of the rooms was a book-shelf next to which I saw four- and five-year-old children with Down syndrome sitting on mats with piles of picture books by their sides. As I walked closer I could see that some of them were reading to each other! I stood there watching them and listening in disbelief until Dr. Martha Cook, the director of the program, came over to me. I asked her if the children had memorized the words in the books. But she assured me that they had all been taught to read. As I looked around the classroom I thought that if I hadn't known that these children had disabilities, I would have believed I was in a regular nursery school.

Despite all of the exciting learning taking place in the class-rooms, Dr. Cook was concerned about the dormitory's crumbling walls, which made it impossible to tape up the children's artwork. She worried about the children who were in wheelchairs and how they couldn't get through the door frames that connected some of the rooms. Instead they had to go out into the hall and down to the next room's main entrance to travel from room to room. Each classroom had only one electrical outlet, making it impossible to plug in a tape recorder for music or more than one lamp, especially during the summer months when the small, inefficient window air conditioners had to be plugged in. That afternoon Ruth Ann and I met many of the children's parents as they came in to pick them up and take them home for the day. Some of them told me how well the program was preparing their children to go on to regular schools. I thought back to my days in Dallas and remembered many meetings where the parents voiced concern about mainstream-ing, and I asked one of the teachers how many of the children at RISE actually went on to regular schools. Her reply, that 90 percent were attending their neighborhood public schools, was astound-ing. Seventy percent of that number would end up in regular kin-dergarten, and only 10 percent of the RISE children would end up in special education classes like Johnny had attended. Mainstreaming, which had seemed so controversial and on the cutting edge nearly twenty years before, was apparently commonplace now. Ruth Ann and I were awed by what we had seen that day, and as we left the RISE program and walked through the quad I said to her, "Can you imagine if Johnny had been able to attend a school like that?"

I paid more frequent visits to RISE and started to learn more about its history. On October 1, 1974, RISE had begun, serving six children with cerebral palsy in one classroom, with a teacher and a teacher's aide. The program began as a federal grant and was funded for fifty thousand dollars as a part of what was then described as the First Chance Network. This grant competition began at the time when deinstitutionalization was receiving prominent media exposure and was established to help families and prevent institutionalization. This was happening just as Johnny was starting school in Dallas and around the same time that the federal educational law was passed.

At that time, RISE was located in an old Victorian house on the edge of campus. The children's classroom was once the formal dining room and still housed a baby grand piano. There was also an adult program in the house — twelve full-grown people with cerebral palsy who were in wheelchairs. But in order for the adults to go out to the bathroom or the kitchen to eat they had to pass through the room with the children in it. Despite all this, Dr. Cook felt that huge strides were being made in the children's learning. The Victorian house has since been torn down and a street now bisects the spot where the program began.

Then in 1976, RISE moved to another old home, again on the fringe of campus, but they had this house all to themselves. On Thomas Street the RISE family expanded to two classrooms located in the living room and the bedroom, and finally they had their very own kitchen and bathroom. They also had a big shady tree where the sixteen children and the six staff members could enjoy an afternoon outdoors. A year later, in 1977, RISE got the news that the program would be moving for the third time, to what would be a bigger facility with four classrooms, in Wilson Hall. Soon enough space would once again become a problem. The number of referrals to the RISE program of children with disabilities tripled from 1981, when the Druid City Hospital upgraded its Neonatal Intensive Care Unit, to 1990. With improvements in medical technology, more babies were surviving, but it seemed a greater percentage had disabilities.

Now RISE had a much broader definition. The program, free to all families, is tailor-made to meet the needs of every infant, toddler, or preschooler who comes there, no matter what his or her disability, whether cerebral palsy, spina bifida, or Down syndrome. Non-disabled children also attend RISE five days a week for six hours a day. The program's goal is to prepare children to go to their neighborhood schools when possible.

As the 1990 season approached I was eager to prove to the media, fans, and players that we would have a winning season. But then after losing three games in a row, I became wary and tense. I would make short visits to RISE in between meetings to make sure one of my players, who had volunteered in the infant room as part of his coursework, had shown up at the center. The word "great" was used for this player from day one. But he had had some well-publicized troubles with the law while in high school and in Alabama. It had taken him a while to get used to the sudden fame and all the attention, both good and bad, and he had had some trouble dealing with it. I'd go into Wilson Hall and watch him, marveling at how gently he fed the babies and then rocked them to sleep. He had a peaceful look as he stopped their crying, laid them in their cribs, and covered them with blankets. During the week I'd keep

198

those contradictory images of him sitting in a rocking chair and singing lullabies to babies as they drifted off to sleep while on Saturdays he would run over people and set records for the Tide. He especially pleased me when he spoke at the RISE graduation in 1990. As the children dressed in little white caps and gowns filed past us, I leaned over and asked him to say a few words to the group of 250 guests. Without any rehearsing, he stood up and said that he had loved working with the children and that they had made him all the more aware of his talents and gifts as an athlete. His compelling speech was well received, and when he finished the audience broke into applause that seemed to last two or three minutes. He handled speaking before the group as smoothly as he did sidestepping a would-be tackler.

By the end of my second season, I knew the players were serious about winning. We had come in 11–1–0, had shut out Georgia and Tulane, and won our bowl game against Colorado. Morale was great and some people were saying that this was the beginning of one of the best defenses in college football history. Defensive linemen Eric Curry and John Copeland and defensive back George Teague were being discovered and ultimately became first-round draft picks for the NFL in 1993. All season Johnny had been following these players and others closely, and now when he came to the games he brought Bradley along and introduced him to the players and told him what position each played. The players soon got to know Bradley almost as well as they knew Johnny. Sometimes I'd take both young men over to RISE with me when I visited. I wanted to go over there as often as I could, because it was such a stimulating, happy environment, and my visits always helped get my mind off the pressures of my work.

One afternoon when Johnny, Bradley, and I were visiting RISE, an adorable little blond girl who couldn't have been more than a foot and a half tall caught my eye, and as I bent down to talk to her she yanked on my tie, bringing me down to her eye level, and said, "Hey, I've seen you on television!" Her name was Sarah Berry, and she was much smaller than the other children because she had dwarfism. She was totally self-confident and full of life, and I found out that she had just gotten off an oxygen tank leash that she had been on ever since she was born. That day Dr. Cook told me that through the Betty Shirley Employment Program young people like Johnny and Bradley would soon be able to be teacher's aides and work directly in the classroom with the RISE children. This was a dream I'd never had for Johnny, and when I talked to Baila, Bradley's mother, she agreed that this kind of job, where Bradley would work with children in an educational setting, went beyond her highest aspirations for him.

In May 1992, the university announced a five-year capital campaign to raise $165 million. A new facility for RISE was one of the priorities. The University of Alabama development office was working with RISE to orchestrate a well-organized campaign to solicit gifts. The university has always provided, and still does provide RISE with 50 percent of its funding. But much more was needed if RISE was going to create the building of its dreams. Betty Shirley provided invaluable support in this effort, hosting luncheons and tirelessly telling the RISE story over and over again. The first donation was for twenty-five thousand dollars, and they were on their way. During the football season that year when I would tape my Sunday morning television show, in addition to discussing the injuries and plays of the game the day before, I started appealing to people for donations to RISE.

One year later, after we had won the national championship, RISE had raised $800,000, about halfway to their $1.6 million goal. The largest gift was from a friend of mine, Pete Hanna, a Birmingham businessman. I had told Pete about RISE and shown him a short film about it and almost right away he had generously donated $300,000.

Meanwhile, some of the friends with whom Johnny worked at PALK, including Bradley, were now getting jobs at RISE. Kevin Kendrick, who was ten years younger than Johnny, worked closely with the toddlers. Kevin, who has Down's, was just enough younger than Johnny that he had learned to read at an early age, and one of his favorite assignments was reading to the children and helping them learn their numbers and helping to dress and feed them. Johnny's younger friend Gina Noland, who had Down's, also spent hours reading to the children. The toddlers would seek Kevin and Gina out; it was if there were a special bond between them. Johnny very much wanted to work there, too. But his job counselor, Terrence Witherspoon, and Ruth Ann and I felt that the work might be too strenuous. His friends had to lift the toddlers and infants and sometimes the atmosphere was noisy and chaotic.

Besides, Terrence, unbeknownst to Ruth Ann and me, had recommended Johnny to work at the Bear Bryant Museum. He contacted the director of the museum, Ken Gaddy, to make sure they could place Johnny. Ken was interested and said yes, but he later told me that because he didn't know Johnny well at the time he had been somewhat hesitant about his capabilities. Finally, one afternoon, Ruth Ann received a call that the museum wanted Johnny as an employee. She was told that he would be working from eight to twelve every morning and that he would be responsible for turning on and off the audiovisual equipment, the VCRs and their monitors, the audiotape players, and the interactive computers and cleaning the glass exhibits each day. They also thought he would be good at giving tours of the museum. Ruth Ann and I talked that evening and we were excited for Johnny. This was the kind of job we had both been wanting for him. It would be so much more interesting than performing the rote duties that he had done for so many years. We had no doubt he would be really good at giving the tours, but we were afraid that people might not be able to understand his slurred speech.

ANOTHER SEASON

In the fall of 1993, Johnny began his new job. His first few weeks on the job were like any new employee's. Ken and the staff wondered if he could do the job, and it took Johnny some time to learn the ropes. His job counselor came with him the first few weeks but eventually phased his visits out so that he only oversaw Johnny occasionally. Johnny insisted on being at the museum on time and he was never late. He got along well with others and did his job well, especially when it came time to give tours. Pretty soon the museum started receiving letters from people saying how much they had liked meeting Johnny Stallings and going on one of his tours.

When he finished his workday, I would often ask someone at the football office to pick him up at the museum and bring him across the street so that he could have lunch with me. This was such a calming time of day for me. To the outsider being a football coach is glamorous, but in reality it is nothing but all-consuming hard work. I could easily get so swept up in the world of football that I could sometimes think of nothing else. But no matter how busy or distracted I was, the minute my son walked into the door and gave me a hug, everything was suddenly all right. After lunch, I would take Johnny's shoes off, and he would lie right down on the sofa in my office. I'd cover him with his favorite blanket and he would instantly fall asleep. While the telephone rang and assistant coaches ran in and out of my office, Johnny would be sound asleep on his back, his arms crossed over his chest, looking as peaceful as a newborn baby.

By late fall the campaign appeared to be at a standstill and it seemed that a new building for RISE would be a distant long-term goal. Then in December they had a site dedication to stimulate interest in the project, which gave the campaign new momentum. The new building was to be on the eastern part of the campus and across the street from Druid City Hospital. On the Sunday before the event, Dr. Cook received a call at home from the vice president in charge of development, Marion Peavy, telling her to sit down. Pete Hanna had decided to finish off the campaign by donating a million dollars. The site dedication instantly became a groundbreaking ceremony. The news was so sudden and so overwhelming that it took a few hours to sink in, and then the RISE staff frantically went out to purchase shovels, painting them gold and tying them with red ribbons on the handles.

Ruth Ann had gone to New York with friends but I agreed to attend the ceremony and say a few words to the crowd. It turned out to be a beautiful mild winter day. All the RISE children were at the site, running and playing, and for some reason they sensed the excitement of our secret announcement. As Pete's helicopter neared the site, the children stopped and waved. I was so grateful to Pete, and as he descended from the chopper, I happily followed him to the podium. Little did I realize that he would have yet another surprise. He announced that the name of the building would be the Stallings Center to honor our family's commitment to people with disabilities. I fought back tears. Now it was my turn to speak to the crowd. I was so moved and honored that I addressed the crowd in a hushed tone, and as I spoke I barely recognized my own voice.

I had thought that raising money would be the hard part. In January, the building was not even a blueprint, but the RISE staff was determined to be in their new home during the 1994 football season, a short nine months away. Dr. Cook appointed a committee that met at the football offices. Although I was in the middle of recruiting athletes, I wanted to attend each meeting to see if I could help. But as the time drew nearer there were a series of little hitches that made it look like the building wouldn't be completed earlier than 1995.

In the summer of 1994, five-year-old Sarah Berry, standing about two feet tall, told the parents gathered for the graduation ceremonies at RISE. "My name is Sarah Berry and I will be going to Verner Elementary School." She had had major back surgery just a few weeks previously and she was in a body cast. The doctors said that she shouldn't be on her feet, but she had insisted on speaking. I was at the farm during the ceremony, but Pete Hanna later told me that he had attended the graduation and was moved to tears by Sarah's speech.

As summer started the building had actually begun to take shape, and as the 1994 football season began I visited the site on Fridays before games and became fascinated by the workmanship that was going into the building. By October, interior walls had gone up and the 1994 target date had become a possibility. The builders shared the sense of urgency and worked overtime to meet our deadline so the program could move in. The program closed Thanksgiving week to make the move.

In designing the building the RISE board had wanted to create a structure that would operate as a preschool but would provide the look and feel of a home. The sweetness and innocence of the children's faces inspired the designers to feature cherubs in the foyer and the private garden. Altogether there were six spacious classrooms, a library, an evaluation room, offices, a workroom, a conference room, and a huge commons. The commons alone had the same square footage as the program's entire previous living quarters. They also had a two-acre fenced-in playground where the children could experience freedom like they'd never had at Wilson Hall.

On the big opening day, Ruth Ann and I met with Pete Hanna, Betty Shirley, and Dr. Roger Sayers, the president of the university, and other friends of RISE at our brand-new building to greet the children. As I walked up the driveway, I saw a small concrete monument in front of the building that said, "THE STALLINGS CENTER, HOME OF THE RISE CENTER." As I read the sign a few times, the word "HOME" jumped out at me. I was deeply moved by it all, especially the children and their families, and I couldn't stop smiling. Some of the children marched right up to me and said, "Hi, Coach Stallings!" At one point Johnny took the microphone and thanked everyone for coming.

The next week we even received national TV exposure. ABC-TV sports commentator Keith Jackson featured the RISE Center during halftime of the SEC championship game. Later, *Good Morning America* profiled Johnny and the Stallings Center during its New Year's Day edition, before our victory the next day at the Florida Citrus Bowl against Ohio State. Unexpectedly, that game marked the final chapter in the football career of Kareem McNeal, our six-foot-six-inch offensive tackle. Six months later on July 3, 1995, I received the news that Kareem had been in a terrible automobile accident the day before, and I immediately flew to Tuscaloosa from the farm to check on him. He had suffered a devastating spinal cord injury that left him paralyzed in a wheelchair. But with the encouragement of his wife and family Kareem continued to be optimistic and strong, and he was able to finish his college degree. He was also determined to walk again. He enrolled in graduate school and then got a job as a graduate assistant at RISE. I recommended him for the job because I felt that he would be a good role model for the children and the positive atmosphere at RISE would be good for Kareem. There, he began his second career and became a favorite with the children.

Exactly one month after Kareem's automobile accident, I received some more bad news. The NCAA Committee on Infractions handed down harsh sanctions against our athletic department for a lack of institutional control. It was a difficult fall as I struggled to understand how something like that could have happened on my watch. Johnny was subdued as he sensed my frustration. I'd find myself going over to RISE more frequently and visiting with the children.

An unusual new pet was also a comfort for me. When I was coaching for the Cowboys I had looked through the want ads for a baby raccoon without any luck. An Alabama fan learned of this and arranged to have one delivered to me. He was a cute little baby and I would get up in the middle of the night and feed him with a bottle. I named him Gerald Jackoon, after my friend Gerald Jack, and I built him a large "coondominium" in our backyard. I grew very attached to the raccoon but he grew quite large and preferred running around the house to staying in his cage. Johnny didn't particularly like him. So one day I took him out to the farm and released him on the property. In November we appealed the sanctions that had been imposed against us, which were then repealed; we became the first NCAA institution in history to be successful in an appeal.

During the 1996 season I continued to visit the sparkling new RISE building frequently and I especially liked watching Kareem working with the children. Many of the babies at RISE were so small they'd practically fit in the palm of his enormous hand. He especially loved the infants and I'd see him singing them lullabies and rocking them to sleep. The toddlers were crazy about him, too, and would jump up on his wheelchair wanting a ride and reaching out to this big man for a hug. It seemed as though a steady stream of visitors came in and out of the building. Some had been visitors to the Bear Bryant Museum who were then adding RISE to their itinerary. Others were interested in disability and traveled from other states, some even from other countries.

We'd had a good season, but an unfortunate loss to Mississippi State hit us hard. The next week's game, the finale against our big rival Auburn, was always a tough game, and there were usually press conferences all week before the game. I paid a few short visits to RISE that week and found that the minute I walked in the door and saw the smiling, radiant faces of the children the tension I had been storing up slowly disappeared.

Auburn and the University of Alabama, both state schools, have been engaged in a fierce rivalry that has intensified over the last thirty years. If you live in the state, it seems you are either for Auburn, on the eastern side of the state, or Alabama, on the western side. In July the fans start talking about the game. If your team loses you spend the whole year thinking how you might turn that around next year. Conversely, if your team wins, you spend most of the year bragging. On the Thursday afternoon before the Auburn game, we were having our usual team meeting when the door opened and there stood Kareem McNeal with crutches under his arms and braces on his legs, his wheelchair pushed away, wearing his old team jersey, number 74. The players turned and looked at him and then gasped. He slowly walked into the room, about fifteen or twenty steps. I could see that his arms were strained from supporting his large frame. He stopped in the center of the room and sweat broke out on his forehead. He looked at the players and said, "I've worked hard to get to this point, and I'm going to throw these braces and crutches away someday. Now you all have worked hard, too, so go out there and beat Auburn!" I, along with the players, broke into tears, and then we all started cheering and clapping. I had known that even though the doctors said Kareem would never walk again he had been receiving therapy and making great progress. Every week he would get out of his wheelchair and go a few feet farther than he had the week before. The players had no idea that he was progressing so well, and I thought it would motivate them to see his incredible courage and drive.

The team dedicated the game to Kareem, who watched from his wheelchair on the ramp behind the south end zone.

It was our home game, played in Legion Field, in Birmingham, and as we warmed up, all I could see was a sea of red and white in the stands. A packed house of over eighty thousand people, mostly Alabama fans, were on their feet screaming as Auburn kicked off to begin the game. Emotions were skyrocketing on our first possession as running back Curtis Alexander caught a short pass from quarterback Freddie Kitchens and ran 64 yards for a touchdown. By the end of the first quarter we had scored again on a short pass from Kitchens to Michael Vaughn and on a field goal by Jon Brock to lead 17–3.

No matter what the score is you can never get comfortable during an Alabama–Auburn game. Sure enough, we turned the ball over five times and Auburn led at halftime 20–17. Auburn added a field goal and led 23–17 going into the fourth quarter. As the players ran to the other side of the field they held up four fingers indicating the fourth quarter would be ours. I certainly hoped so. The fans were on their feet screaming as the teams took turns moving down the field. When it looked like one team would go in and score, the other team would come up with an unbelievable defensive play. With 2:14 left we had no time-outs remaining. This was it; we had to not only score but score a touchdown and make the extra point to win. As the team went into a huddle, one of the players looked up and saw Kareem cheering. "We've just got to win," he told his teammates and pointed to Kareem.

We started from our 26 yard line. After some great runs and passes and an interference penalty on Auburn we had driven the ball down to the Auburn 8 yard line. First down with thirty-two seconds left. On the next play Kitchens threw the ball and he scampered in for the touchdown. The players were celebrating, but all I could think of was getting them off the field to get that extra point to win the game. Jon Brock kicked it through, putting us ahead 24–23. But I didn't really feel comfortable because I knew that Auburn was capable of coming up with some big plays. Each time their quarterback threw the ball our defensive backs rose to the challenge and tipped the ball away. As the clock ran out their quarterback threw a Hail Mary pass that was knocked away, and the game was over. I watched the players as they pointed their fingers toward

Kareem at the end zone, signifying that we had won the game. It wasn't until later that I realized that we had gone 74 yards to score the final touchdown. Ironically, 74 was Kareem's number.

I was full of all sorts of emotions. The pure joy of winning the game lasted only a few minutes because of the burden I felt of making the announcement that I would be resigning as head coach of Alabama. Moments later I faced the press and declared I was leaving. I had always known the Alabama fans had a passionate spirit in whatever they believed in, but I'd had no idea that I would grow to love them as much as I did or that they would provide Johnny with the kind of support and lifestyle that would sustain our whole family for seven years. This was a very tough and emotional decision for me that I wrestled with over the last few weeks of the season. But I had watched Johnny slow down. He took a long time to get from one place to another, and he became more and more emotional every time we lost a game. I started thinking that my family might be happier without the constant highs and lows of a football family's life. With a new athletic director and president at the university, this was the perfect time to pass the torch on to someone else.

Although I had a year remaining on my contract, I had signed a clause that said that I could leave at any time. I had accomplished much of what I wanted. The Stallings Center was up and running, and over the last seven seasons I had compiled an average of almost ten wins a season. I would be leaving with a 70–15–1 record and a national championship. As I spoke at my press conference I said that it was time to close this chapter of my life and pass the torch on to someone else. Maybe someday I would go back into coaching. But for now Johnny needed me. As I finished speaking I looked over at him sitting next to his two sisters, Martha Kate and Jackie, and he was sobbing. I put my arm around him and said, "Let's go home, son."

As we left the stadium that night photographers and reporters trailed us. As the lights of their cameras flashed and the reporters yelled out their questions they were just as anxious to get Johnny's picture, comments, and reactions as they were mine. That Monday at work I opened up the *Birmingham Post-Herald* and there on the back page of the sports section was a half-page color photograph of John Mark crying as I announced my resignation. I read the accompanying news story and saw that much of the article focused on Johnny. I propped my feet up on my desk, folded up my newspaper, and thought back to those few hours leading up to the national championship game on New Year's Day 1993 and how Johnny, Ruth Ann, and the girls had left the Riverwalk Hilton before me. I didn't know it at the time, but Johnny had described to me later that night how after the game he had got off the elevator before his mother and sisters, and when the lobby crowds — eight and ten people deep — saw him they began a chant that lasted for fifteen minutes. Security had started to surround Johnny. It wasn't "Roll, Tide!" they were chanting but "Johnny! Johnny! Johnny!" The fans had held out notebooks and scraps of paper and asked for Johnny's autograph. I rested my head against the back of my chair and closed my eyes. I saw him carefully signing his name and facing those fans in the hotel lobby, his fingers forming the victory sign. Ruth Ann had told me how he was smiling and laughing, basking in the jubilation of the crowd, strutting around the lobby saying, "We're number one!"

There was a loud knock on my office door, which startled me, and I took my feet off the desk and pitched the newspaper into the trash. "Come on in!" I called. It was Johnny. He was ready for his lunch and a nap. He stood in the doorway and I thought how handsome he looked in his crimson sweater. I went over to him, smoothed his cowlicks down with the back of my hand, and then embraced him for a long time. "Good job, son!" I whispered.

EPILOGUE

A DREAM FULFILLED

SIX weeks after I announced that I was leaving Alabama, the staff of the Paul Bryant Museum hosted a farewell reception in Johnny's honor. It was a cold January evening and Ruth Ann and I stood over to the side of the expansive lobby watching as people streamed in the front door. My footsteps had always sounded so hollow on the lobby's granite floor, but tonight the warm chatter and laughter of Johnny's guests filled the room. I watched as people spilled over to the exhibit area, a space where photographs and memorabilia of all the great Alabama coaches, particularly Coach Bryant, create an overwhelming sense of history. It is a place where people come to share in a kind of ownership of a tradition that makes them proud, the perfect spot for Johnny's farewell party.

Two hundred people were invited and over three hundred showed up. Johnny, looking poised and confident, worked the room like a pro as he introduced his friends to one another. I saw his pals from PALK and RISE, his friends from church, and people from the athletic office. Andrew Sorenson, the new president of the university, was there, and so were Johnny's barbers, Don Whitley and Dennis Elmore, his confidants who had cut his hair for the last seven years. Paul Bryant Jr. and Bradley Block came, and there were many people from all walks of life who had disabilities. Everyone who was invited meant something to Johnny and he remembered the names of all the guests — some of whom he hadn't seen in at least five years.

I had always been deeply appreciative of his work at the museum, the most meaningful job in his life. Without being taxed physically, he had used his knowledge of football and audiovisual equipment, and certainly his strong people talents were all put to good use leading tours and making friends with the staff at the museum. During the last three and a half years I had seen his confidence soar. Clearly, he had been the happiest I had ever seen him.

Through his job, he had become a vital figure in Tuscaloosa and had affected large numbers of people who came in contact with him. Kenneth Gaddy, the director of the museum, told me that night how he had never spent much time around anyone who had a disability. When Johnny first arrived he thought that Johnny might not be able to perform his job well. But Johnny proved to him that he was responsible, and it didn't take Kenneth long to see how Johnny touched the lives of almost everyone he met with his kind and gentle nature. Kenneth told me how much Johnny had taught him and the whole staff.

Now when the staff goes out to a restaurant or other public place, they check to see if it is wheelchair accessible. When there are new exhibits at the museum, Kenneth thinks of the people passing through who may have a disability and makes adjustments accordingly. There had never been more traffic through the museum than in the past three years, and Ken believed that Johnny had something to do with that.

Standing over in the corner, watching Johnny hugging his

friends, smiling and posing for photographers, I thought back to the chronic sorrow I had experienced when my son was first born and the obsessive thoughts I had that he would be ostracized and ridiculed, ultimately living a life where only our family would learn to value him. I remembered back to the veil of secrecy surrounding his early months, how few people asked about him and behind our backs pitied us.

As Johnny mingled easily with the guests, I reflected how much he had influenced others' attitudes, helping to open doors for people with disabilities. His warm, friendly manner has drawn people from all walks of life to him, and he has demonstrated that he can hold a job and work hard. His interest in music and sports provides a common bond with the many people he meets, and he has shown me and countless others that indeed we are more alike than different from one another.

As the night was coming to an end I watched Johnny saying his final farewells. Amid photographs of football greats and showcases of football paraphernalia, I noticed a plaque to his right with a famous quote from Coach Bryant that read: "If you believe in yourself and have dedication and pride and never quit you'll be a winner. The price of victory is high but so are the rewards." In thirty-four short years Johnny had gone from an object of pity, someone to be locked up in an institution, to a man who was not only loved but valued by countless people. It was a dream night and it was all Johnny's.

ACKNOWLEDGMENTS

▼

We have had tremendous encouragement and support while writing this book. Special thanks to Laurence Bergreen, a keen and wise biographer, who believed in this story from the start and helped make it a reality. At Little, Brown, Catherine Crawford not only demonstrated her talent with words but was also unwavering in her sense of what this book should be. Bill Phillips's clear and thoughtful suggestions on improving the manuscript were extremely helpful. Working with both Catherine and Bill was a privilege. Thank you to David Coen for his interest and careful attention to detail, and to Chip Rossetti for keeping things moving smoothly.

In Tuscaloosa, Linda Knowles, who began her career in the Alabama football office in 1961 working with Coach Bryant and later with Coach Stallings, provided exceptional help. In the course of her hectic workday she always found time to answer any question, no matter how mundane. She offered invaluable suggestions, insight, and understanding. Dr. Martha Cook (no relation to the coauthor) rigorously read the manuscript and contributed excellent

ACKNOWLEDGMENTS

advice on every aspect of the book, providing information and background about disability laws. Her infinite compassion toward the children, families, staff members, teachers, and supporters of the RISE program was a constant source of inspiration. Betty Shirley and Baila Block spoke to us for hours about Walter Gary's and Bradley Block's lives while explaining the importance of meaningful work for people with disabilities. The staff of the Paul Bryant Museum — Kenneth Gaddy, Clem Gryska, Taylor Watson, Gary Shores, and Jan Adams — provided us with important tools: a workspace, the use of their copier, and access to archives. From an employer's perspective Kenneth gave us new insights into Johnny. Barry Allen and Larry White from the University of Alabama athletic department helped jog our memories when it came to statistics and game scores. Thank you to our imaginative literary agents, Anne Dubuisson and Elizabeth Kaplan from the Ellen Levine Literacy Agency, for their thorough attention to every phase and detail of this project. Thanks to Jaymie Meyer for meticulous transcribing.

This book could not have been written without the help of our friends and family. Ruth Ann Stallings cheerfully opened up her heart and mind and dedicated tireless hours to talk about her family and what it is like to raise a child with a disability. To her we owe more than we can say. Bob Cook lent suggestions, criticism, and assistance whenever and however they were needed. Once again he proved to be an editor, father, and husband extraordinaire. From Anna Lee Young, Laurie Vanderpool, Jackie Chalk, and Martha Kate Gunn we heard stories about growing up with their brother, Johnny. They confirmed the power of love among siblings. Jean Durgan, Daniel Williams, M.D., and John Williams, M.D., read the manuscript and offered valuable suggestions. Diane McWhorter shared her zeal for Alabama football and her extensive knowledge of her native state, and Stacey Farley helped launch the project. Thank you to both of them for their continued interest and friendship. Michael Globetti and Michael Moschen each read the manuscript, lending excellent comments and ideas. Jean and Felix Gibson and Gerald Jack, as always, provided laughter, assistance whenever it was needed, and enduring friendship.

We are equally grateful to other individuals who generously shared their thoughts, recollections, and encouragement. They include: Peaches Allen and her family, Scott Anderson, Patricia Ardila, Andrea Barnet, Sheryle Bolton, Angie Prince Brooks, the Dale Bumpers family, Cedric Burns, Peter Canby, Luis Canedo, M.D., Sara Canedo, Laura Cornell, John Coston, Peter Davoren, George Dillman, Arlene Goldsmith, Cliff Harris, Jane Hicks, Isabelle Holland, Lee Roy Jordan, Henry Kallan, Jim Lampley, Tom Landry, Colette Linnihan, Danielle Mailer, Kate Manning, Bill McDonald, Kate and Jim McMullan, Lucia Nevai, Roberta Oster, Luisa Pavon, Barbara Peterson, Anne Putnam, Larry and Wendy Rockefeller, Richard Rosen, Steve Shane, Amy Short, Lol Sloan, Mary Somoza and family, Bridget Taylor, Charlotte and Adam Van Doren, Barbara von Bulow, Lee Wade, Bree Walker, Charlie Waters, and Kit White. And to our many other supportive friends in Tuscaloosa, Alabama; Paris, Texas; New York City; and Cornwall, Connecticut — thank you.

Printed in the United States
55729LVS00004B/4